Getting to Know
Connected Mathematics

A Guide to the
Connected Mathematics
Curriculum

Lappan, Fey, Fitzgerald, Friel, and Phillips

Dale Seymour Publications®

The Connected Mathematics Project was developed at Michigan State University with financial support from the Michigan State University Office of the Provost, Computing and Technology, and the College of Natural Science.

This material is based upon work supported by the National Science Foundation under Grant No. MDR 9150217.

This project was supported, in part, by the
National Science Foundation
Opinions expressed are those of the authors and not necessarily those of the Foundation

Connected Mathematics Project
101 Wills House
Michigan State University
East Lansing, Michigan 48824-1050
517-336-2870

This book is published by Dale Seymour Publications®, an imprint of Addison Wesley Longman, Inc.

Dale Seymour Publications
10 Bank Street
White Plains, NY 10602
Customer Service: 800-872-1100

DALE
SEYMOUR
PUBLICATIONS®

Order number DS45715
ISBN 1-57232-438-4

3 4 5 6 7 8 9 - VGR - 02 01 00 99 98

This Book is Printed
on Recycled Paper

Project Directors
James T. Fey, University of Maryland
William M. Fitzgerald, Michigan State University
Susan N. Friel, University of North Carolina
Glenda Lappan, Michigan State University
Elizabeth Difanis Phillips, Michigan State University

Project Manager
Kathy Burgis, Michigan State University

Technical Coordinator
Judith Martus Miller, Michigan State University

Collaborating Teacher/Writers
Mary K. Bouck, Portland, Michigan
Jacqueline Stewart, Okemos, Michigan

Curriculum Development Consultants
David Ben-Chaim, Weizmann Institute
Alex Friedlander, Weizmann Institute
Eleanor Geiger, University of Maryland
Jane Mitchell, University of North Carolina
Anthony D. Rickard, Alma College

Graduate Assistants
Scott J. Baldridge, Michigan State University
Angie S. Eshelman, Michigan State University
M. Faaiz Gierdien, Michigan State University
Jane M. Keiser, Indiana University
Angela S. Krebs, Michigan State University
James M. Larson, Michigan State University
Ronald Preston, Indiana University
Tat Ming Sze, Michigan State University
Sarah Theule-Lubienski, Michigan State University
Jeffrey J. Wanko, Michigan State University

Graphic Design Team
Katherine Oesterle, Michigan State University
Stacy Otto, University of North Carolina

Evaluation Team
Diana V. Lambdin, Indiana University (Project Evaluator)
Sandra K. Wilcox, Michigan State University
Judith S. Zawojewski, National-Louis University

Teacher/Assessment Team
Kathy Booth, Waverly, Michigan
Anita Clark, Marshall, Michigan
Theodore Gardella, Bloomfield Hills, Michigan
Yvonne Grant, Portland, Michigan
Linda R. Lobue, Vista, California
Suzanne McGrath, Chula Vista, California
Nancy McIntyre, Troy, Michigan
Linda Walker, Tallahassee, Florida

Software Developer
Richard Burgis, East Lansing, Michigan

This project was supported, in part,
by the
National Science Foundation
Opinions expressed are those of the authors
and not necessarily those of the Foundation

PREFACE

The *Connected Mathematics Project (CMP)* was funded by the National Science Foundation to develop a complete mathematics curriculum with teacher support materials for the Middle Grades, 6, 7, and 8. This curriculum is devoted to developing student knowledge and understanding of mathematics that is rich in connections—connections among core ideas in mathematics, connections between mathematics and its applications in other school subjects, connections between the planned teaching/learning activities and the special aptitudes and interests of middle school students, connections among the mathematics strands of a modern elementary and secondary school program, and connections with the applications of mathematical ideas in the world outside school.

Observations of patterns and relationships lie at the heart of acquiring deep understanding in mathematics. Therefore, the curriculum is organized around interesting problem settings—real situations, whimsical situations, or interesting mathematical situations. Students solve problems and in so doing they observe patterns and relationships; they conjecture, test, discuss, verbalize, and generalize these patterns and relationships. Clearly, this calls for an instructional model in the classroom that encourages higher level thinking and problem solving and that has, at its core, making sense of mathematics and its uses.

This booklet is designed to help you get to know the *CMP* materials. You will find sections that give the overall mathematical goals of the project. Other sections describe in detail the features of the student materials and the teacher materials including a discussion of an instructional model that is built into the teacher support materials. We hope that you will find the booklet helpful as you examine *CMP* for the first time, as well as during your first years of teaching *CMP* materials. All the suggestions in this booklet are meant as just that—suggestions. We recognize and appreciate that all teachers as professionals make instructional decisions that are in the best interest of their particular students. We hope you will view all *CMP* materials—student and teacher materials—as giving a set of possibilities from which you as the reflective teacher will craft your own instructional practice. We also hope that you will find the set of possibilities that we have provided to be extremely useful as you work to build mathematical power for all your students.

I. The *CMP* Curriculum:

MATHEMATICAL CONTENT AND PROCESS GOALS FOR *CMP*

In designing a complete and connected middle school mathematics curriculum, it is not possible to separate the influence of *what* is taught from *how* it is taught. *What students learn* from the curriculum, i.e., the *mathematical content* of the curriculum, is shaped by how they learn to work with mathematics, i.e., the *mathematical processes* embedded in the curriculum. Conversely, *how students learn to use mathematics* shapes what they learn about mathematics and how concepts are understood and related.

The specific mathematical content and process goals of *CMP* are provided below. Although they are presented separately, the section following the content and process goals illustrates how they are entwined with a snapshot of a classroom using one of the *CMP* Units.

Mathematical Content Goals

Number   Number sense and reasoning with and about numbers; number theory; properties and operations of number systems, with focus on integers and rational numbers; number estimation; ratio, proportion, and percentage; representation of numbers in concrete, graphic, and symbolic forms; scientific notation; and exponential notation.

Geometry   Spatial sense and reasoning with and about shapes and location; two- and three-dimensional shapes and their properties; relations among shapes (congruence, similarity, parallelism, perpendicularity, symmetry); location; coordinate systems; transformations; visualization, and sketching of shapes.

Measurement   A sense of what it means to measure and to reason with measures; concepts of length, area, volume, mass, angle measure; common properties of measurement systems; procedures for exact, approximate, and derived measurements; estimation.

Algebra	Algebraic reasoning; variables, patterns and functions, relations; modeling, representation by symbolic expressions, numerical tables, and graphs; equations and inequalities; and rates of change.
Statistics	Decision-making with data; formulating questions, collecting, displaying, analyzing, making inferences from data; and sampling.
Probability	Decision making under uncertainty; random events; equally likely events and unequally likely events; experimental and theoretical probability; expected value; simulation.

The four overarching goals in the *National Council of Teachers in Mathematics (NCTM) Curriculum and Evaluation Standards for School Mathematics*—**Problem Solving, Communication, Reasoning, and Connections**—serve as the major process goals for *CMP*. In addition, *CMP* has the following specific process goals:

Mathematical Process Goals

Count	Determine the number of elements in finite data sets, trees, graphs, or combinations by application of mental computation, estimation, counting principles, calculators and computers, and formal algorithms.
Visualize	Recognize and describe shape, size, and position of one-, two-, and three-dimensional objects and their images under transformations; interpret graphical representations of data, functions, relations, and symbolic expressions.
Compare	Describe relations among quantities and shapes using concepts such as equal, less than, greater than, more or less likely, orders of magnitude, proportions, congruence, similarity, parallelism, perpendicularity, symmetry, and rates of growth or change.
Estimate	Determine reasonableness of answers. Use "benchmark" to estimate measures. Use various strategies to approximate a calculation and to compare estimates.

Measure	Assign numbers as measures of geometric objects, probabilities of events, and choices in a decision-making problem. Choose appropriate units or scales and make approximate measurements or apply formal rules to find measures.
Model	Construct, make inferences from, and interpret concrete, symbolic, graphic, verbal, and algorithmic models of quantitative, visual, statistical, probabilistic, and algebraic relations in problem situations. Translate information from one model to another.
Reason	Bring to any problem situation the disposition and ability to observe, experiment, analyze, abstract, induce, deduce, extend, generalize, relate, manipulate, and prove interesting and important patterns.
Play	Have the disposition and imagination to inquire, investigate, tinker, dream, conjecture, invent, and communicate with others about mathematical ideas.
Use Tools	Select and use intelligently—calculators, computers, drawing tools, and physical models to represent, simulate, and manipulate patterns and relations in problem settings.

CMP student materials are organized into units, each of which focuses on a core set of important, related mathematics ideas. The units develop the above eight process goals in tandem with the content goals for students in each of the five mathematical strands of the *CMP* curriculum.

MATHEMATICAL CONTENT AND PROCESSES

This section examines a vignette from a classroom studying the *CMP* unit *Covering and Surrounding*. The vignette focuses on the teacher's interaction with three of her students about a problem in the unit.

An Argument About the Area of Triangles

Deborah Taylor is a 6th Grade teacher in a large urban school. Ms. Taylor taught the *CMP* unit *Covering and Surrounding*, which is about the measurement concepts of perimeter and area and the relationships between them, in her mathematics class. In the first five investigations of the unit, students build a conceptual understanding of perimeter as the number of linear units required to *surround* a figure and area as the number of square units needed to *cover* a figure. In the fifth and sixth investigations, students begin to use their understanding of area of rectangles to explore area of triangles and parallelograms. After working on Problem 3 of Investigation 6 for a while, a group of three students, Matt, Trevor, and Alicia, were eager to share something with Ms. Taylor. They were excited about a discovery they had made:

Problem 6.3: Draw two triangles on a sheet of grid paper. Make sure the triangles are very different from one another. For each triangle, complete parts a)–c).

a) Record the base, height, area, and perimeter of your triangle.

b) Make a copy of your triangle, and cut out both copies. Experiment with putting the two triangles together to make new polygons. Describe and sketch the polygons that are possible.

c) Can you make a parallelogram by piecing together the two identical triangles? If so, record the base, height, area, and perimeter of the parallelogram. How do these measures compare to the measures of the original triangles?

d) Draw a parallelogram on grid paper, and cut it out. Can you cut the parallelogram into two triangles that are the same shape and size? Describe and sketch what you find.

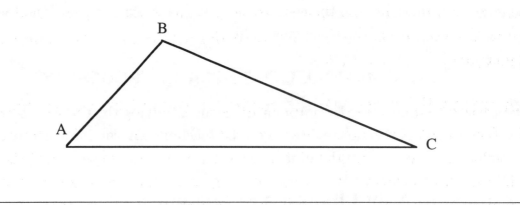

Matt, Trevor, and Alicia showed Ms. Taylor two congruent right triangles that were pushed together to form a rectangle:

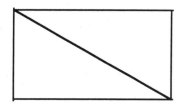

The three students told Ms. Taylor that they had discovered why the area of a triangle was "one-half the base times the height." Ms. Taylor listened closely as the students explained their reasoning to her:

Matt: *Basically, you can make a rectangle from two equal right triangles. The base times the height gives you, like, the area of the rectangle.*

Trevor: *But we want the area of the triangle, not the area of the whole thing— I mean the rectangle. So you just take half of the base times the height because the triangle is half of the rectangle.*

Alicia: *Yea. You can see that it's [indicating triangle] half of it [indicating the rectangle] so you only need half of it—like half of the area of the rectangle.*

Ms. Taylor: *This sounds interesting—good work! What I would like each of you to do is sit down and construct your own explanation—in writing–and showing me your diagram, i.e., the rectangle constructed from two congruent triangles—of this discovery. Tomorrow I'll have you share this with the class.*

Clearly excited at having their discovery recognized, Matt, Trevor, and Alicia went back to their desks and each began writing a description of the reasoning they had just shared with Ms. Taylor.

Interaction Between Mathematical Content and Process

Matt, Trevor, and Alicia made a discovery that is a special case of a more general justification for the area formula for triangles. For *any* triangle (not just right triangles), two congruent copies can be put together to form a parallelogram, e.g., a rectangle in the case of right triangles. The area of the parallelogram is the product of the base and height of the triangles that form the figure. This is the case since a parallelogram can always be transformed into a rectangle with dimensions equal to the base and height of the parallelogram and hence the base and height of the triangle.

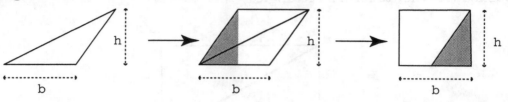

Since the triangle is half the area of the parallelogram, its area is one-half the product of its base and height, i.e., half of the area of the parallelogram.

One could argue that the mathematical content and process embedded in the snapshot from Ms. Taylor's classroom consists of two pieces: (1) The content of the lesson is the discovery and justification of the area formula for a triangle, i.e., $A = \frac{1}{2} \times B \times H$; (2) the process for learning about the area formula is cutting out and rearranging shapes to look for relationships. However, the interaction between content and process yields additional opportunities for students' learning that are also entwined, but perhaps not explicit, in the lesson.

For example, as illustrated in the students' comments, exploring the area formula for triangles through the process of cutting and rearranging shapes helped them make *connections* between areas of triangles and rectangles, e.g., the area of the triangle is half the area of the rectangle. Furthermore, the students used the connection between the area of their triangles and rectangle to explain why the area of a triangle can be found by multiplying one-half the base times the height. Matt, Trevor, and Alicia were also able to *communicate* their findings both verbally and with a diagram; Ms. Taylor also encouraged them to communicate their argument in writing. The three students used the diagram to guide their *reasoning* in deciding if the area formula for triangles was really valid. Using the diagram to explore the area between rectangles and triangles also requires *problem solving* to decide how to cut and rearrange shapes and how to measure the triangle in the same terms as the rectangle, i.e., base and height.

The interaction between the content and process of Matt, Trevor, and Alicia's investigation afforded opportunities for making connections, communicating, reasoning and problem solving as well as cutting and rearranging shapes to learn about finding the area of triangles. These facets of the snapshot from Ms. Taylor's classroom are all important aspects of mathematics that students should have opportunities to develop throughout K–12 mathematics (see NCTM, 1989).

An effective and complete middle school mathematics curriculum must not only provide students with opportunities to learn mathematical content and processes, but must also offer help to teachers to accomplish teaching this curriculum in their mathematics classrooms (cf., NCTM, 1989; NCTM, 1991). To help teachers achieve the vision of teaching connected mathematics, the developers of *CMP* curriculum organize the curriculum around five instructional themes.

INSTRUCTIONAL THEMES OF THE *CONNECTED MATHEMATICS PROJECT*

The *Connected Mathematics Project* materials were written with a philosophy about key instructional themes to guide the development. These themes are tied to the content and process goals, but point more directly to the nature of kinds of classroom discourse needed to support the growth of student understanding and skill.

Teaching for Understanding: The curriculum is organized around mathematical "big ideas," clusters of important, related mathematical concepts, processes, ways of thinking, skills, and problem solving strategies, which are studied in depth with the development of deep understanding as the goal.

Connections: The curriculum emphasizes significant connections among various mathematical topics that are presented and between mathematics and problems in other school subjects that are meaningful to students and offers an opportunity to revisit ideas.

Mathematical Investigations: Instruction emphasizes inquiry and discovery of mathematical ideas through investigation of rich problem situations.

Representations: Students grow in their ability to reason effectively with information represented in graphic, numeric, symbolic, and verbal forms and move flexibly among these representations.

Technology: Selection of mathematical goals and teaching approaches reflects the information processing capabilities of calculators and computers and the fundamental changes such tools are making in the ways people learn mathematics and apply their knowledge to problem solving tasks (Fitzgerald, et al., 1991, p. 3).

These five instructional themes are compatible with criteria for teaching and learning mathematics as described by the NCTM in the *Professional Standards for Teaching Mathematics* (NCTM, 1991) and in the *Curriculum and Evaluation Standards for School Mathematics* (NCTM, 1989).

At each grade level, the *CMP* curriculum is organized into eight units that are four to six weeks in length. The following section looks at these units from several different perspectives.

ORGANIZATION OF THE CURRICULUM

Each grade consists of eight units with each unit developing a major concept or cluster of related concepts. The following table gives an overview of the curriculum at each grade level with short main ideas descriptors.

CMP Curriculum for Grades 6, 7, & 8

6th Grade	7th Grade	8th Grade

Prime Time
Number Theory; primes; composites, factors and multiples

Variables and Patterns
Introducing Algebra; variables, tables, graphs, and symbols as representations

Thinking with Mathematical Models
Introduction to Functions and Modeling

Data About Us
Data Investigation; Formulating questions, gathering data, organizing and analyzing data, making decisions based on data

Stretching and Shrinking
Similarity with congruence as a special case

Looking for Pythagoras
Pythagorean Theorem, slope, area and irrational numbers

Shapes and Designs
Reasoning about shapes and shape properties; angle measure

Comparing and Scaling
Rate, Ratio, Proportion, Percent and Proportional Reasoning

Growing, Growing, Growing...
Exponential Growth

Bits and Pieces, Part I
Understanding Rational Numbers: Fractions, Decimals, and Percents

Accentuate the Negative
Understanding and Using Integers

Frogs, Fleas, and Painted Cubes
Quadratic Growth

Covering and Surrounding
Measurement: Area and Perimeter

Moving Straight Ahead
Linear Relationships expressed in words, tables, graphs, and symbols

Say It With Symbols
Equivalent expressions and solutions of linear equations

How Likely Is It?
Probability

Filling and Wrapping
3-D Measurement

Hubcaps, Kaleidoscopes, and Mirrors!
Transformational Geometry

Bits and Pieces, Part II
Using Rational Numbers: Computation

What Do You Expect?
Probability (Expected Value)

Samples and Populations
Gathering data from samples to make predictions about populations

Ruins of Montarek
Spatial visualization and spatial reasoning

Data Around Us
Number Sense

Clever Counting
Using trees, lists, and principals to count set: combinatorics

Another way to look at the curriculum is to organize the units by mathematical strands. Listed below is a partial classification of the *CMP* units by mathematical strands. Some of the units are hard to classify in terms of the more traditional mathematical strands because they tend to deal with several different strands in a single unit. In this listing a unit is placed in the strand or strands of major emphasis.

In some cases, a unit from another strand provides essential mathematical background. In these cases, the units from outside the strand are indicated by parentheses.

Scope of the *Connected Mathematics* Curriculum by Mathematical Strands

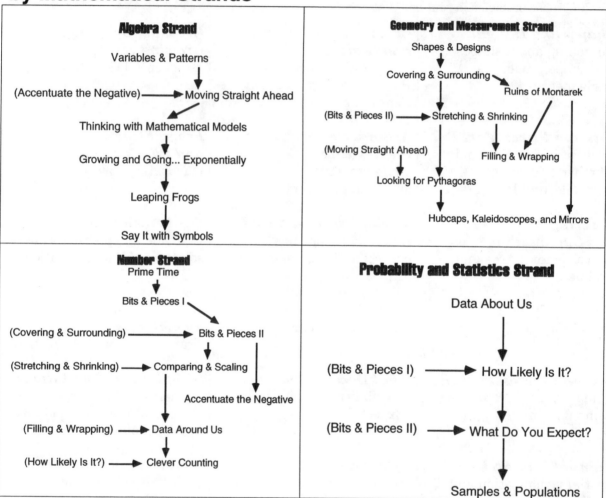

The *Connected Mathematics Project* is designed to meet all the *NCTM Standards* documents—*Curriculum and Evaluation Standards for School Mathematics, Professional Teaching Standards for Mathematics,* and *Assessment Standards for*

Mathematics. This section shows how the *CMP* curriculum is related to all the important areas of mathematics and mathematical thinking advocated by the *NCTM Curriculum and Evaluation Standards for School Mathematics.* In sections on teaching and assessment there is a discussion of how *CMP* is related to the other *Standards* documents.

CMP and the *NCTM Curriculum and Evaluation Standards for School Mathematics*

Standard 1. Mathematics as Problem Solving All the *CMP* units are divided into Investigations which present problems for the students to solve. The entire curriculum is built around these problems in contexts that are interesting to the students. Many of the contexts have validity in the real world. Others use fantasy or mathematics itself as a context.	**Standard 2. Mathematics as Communication** Emphasis is placed on the students discussing the problems in class, talking through their solutions, and learning how to communicate their solutions to a more general audience. They learn how to communicate by using different kinds of representations such as graphs, tables, formulas, or written explanations or arguments.
Standard 3. Mathematics as Reasoning Through discussing the problems and their solutions, the students are learning to reason about the mathematics. They learn that mathematics is man-made, that it is arbitrary, and good solutions are arrived at by consensus among those who are considered expert. The students learn also that this is an activity in which they can be involved in a real way.	**Standard 4. Mathematics as Connections** The name of our project conveys our commitment to connecting the mathematics to other areas of mathematics, and to applications of mathematics in the real world. The investigation problems are set in contexts and the Applications – Connections – Extensions section of each investigation provides time to reflect on connections.
Standard 5. Number and Number Relationships *Bits and Pieces I (Grade 6)* *Bits and Pieces II (Grade 6)* *Comparing and Scaling (Grade 7)* *Accentuate the Negative (Grade 7)* *Data Around Us (Grade 7)*	**Standard 6. Number Systems and Number Theory** *Prime Time (Grade 6)* *Accentuate the Negative (Grade 7)* *Looking for Pythagoras (Grade 8)* *Say It With Symbols (Grade 8)*
Standard 7. Computation and Estimation *Bits and Pieces II (Grade 6)* *Data Around Us (Grade 7)* *Clever Counting (Grade 8)* *Comparing and Scaling (Grade 7)* *Covering and Surrounding (Grade 6)* *Filling and Wrapping (Grade 7)*	**Standard 8. Patterns and Functions** *Variables and Patterns (Grade 7)* *Moving Straight Ahead Grade 7)* *Thinking with Mathematical Models (Grade 8)* *Growing, Growing, Growing... (Grade 8)* *Frogs, Fleas, and Painted Cubes (Grade 8)*

Standard 9. Algebra	**Standard 10. Statistics**
Moving Straight Ahead (Grade 7) *Thinking With Mathematical Models* *(Grade 8)* *Growing, Growing, Growing...Grade 8)* *Say It With Symbols (Grade 8)* *Frogs, Fleas, and Painted Cubes (Grade 8)* *Hubcaps, Kaleidoscopes, and Mirrors! (Grade 8)*	*Data About Us (Grade 6)* *Data Around Us (Grade 7)* *Samples and Populations (Grade 8)*
Standard 11. Probability	**Standard 12. Geometry**
How Likely Is It? (Grade 6) *What Do You Expect? (Grade 7)* *Samples and Populations (Grade 8)* *Clever Counting (Grade 8)*	*Shapes and Designs (Grade 6)* *Ruins of Montarek (Grade 6)* *Stretching and Shrinking (Grade 7)* *Looking for Pythagoras (Grade 8)* *Hubcaps, Kaleidoscopes, and Mirrors!* *(Grade 8)*

Standard 13. Measurement
Shapes and Designs (Grade 6)
Covering and Surrounding (Grade 6)
Filling and Wrapping (Grade 7)
Data Around Us (Grade 7)
Looking for Pythagoras (Grade 8)

Connections Both Within and Across the Units of *CMP*

In designing any curriculum for mathematics, there are many ways to organize the flow of the development of the ideas and concepts. However, because time is linear, there is a prescribed order determined by the order in which units are taught. The consequences of these two ideas—many possible orders, but linear time, is that, of necessity, some unit will be taught before others. *CMP* developers have made a set of decisions about order among units that reflects our commitment to connectedness, yet reflects that teachers must have choices. Since schools do not allot the same amount of time to mathematics across the country, some schools will be able to do all the *CMP* units for each grade level in a year. However, many schools will not be able to use all the units in a given year, especially in the first year or two of using the curriculum.

For some of the key mathematical ideas, the development occurs over several units, sometimes within a grade level and at others across grade levels. For example, developing understanding and skill with using fractions, decimals, percents, ratio, rates, and proportional reasoning is a main goal of several units in Grades 6 and 7. While we could have made different decisions about order, once chosen, we have written the units in the strand so that they build on each other. It would be more difficult for students to study these units in a different order. For other units there is more freedom. For example, the spatial visualization unit, *Ruins of Montarek,* for Grade 6 can be taught almost at any time in any one of the three grades.

To help you with decision for your school that fit your special circumstances (time for mathematics classes, support for teachers in implementing a new curriculum, curriculum goals for the district, etc.), we have developed a diagram for each grade level that shows the units that should be taught in order and the other units that can be taught in a different order or if absolutely necessary, at a different grade level.

The final graphic shows the entire 24 units of *CMP* with connections among unit within and across grades that indicate optimal orders in which the units should be taught. Note that there are units that build across grades. For example, the seventh grade probability unit assumes that the students have either studied the *CMP* Grade 6 probability unit, or comparable material from other sources.

It may be possible for a district, over time, to work toward moving some material from Grade 6 into Grade 5. The *Prime Time* unit and the *Ruins of Montarek* unit can be taught successfully at Grade 5 if the students have been in a program that sets high expectations.

Recommended Order & Unit Connections:

Grade 6: Recommended Order & Unit Connections

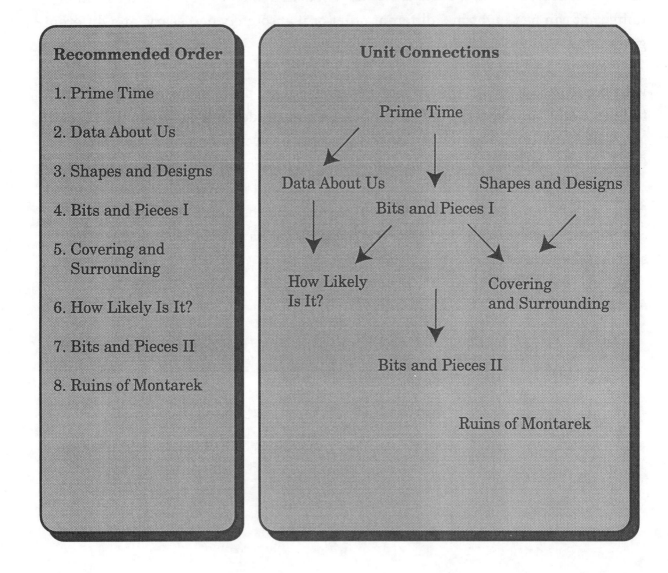

Recommended Order

1. Prime Time

2. Data About Us

3. Shapes and Designs

4. Bits and Pieces I

5. Covering and Surrounding

6. How Likely Is It?

7. Bits and Pieces II

8. Ruins of Montarek

Unit Connections

Prime Time

Data About Us   Shapes and Designs

Bits and Pieces I

How Likely Is It?   Covering and Surrounding

Bits and Pieces II

Ruins of Montarek

Grade 7: Recommended Order & Unit Connections

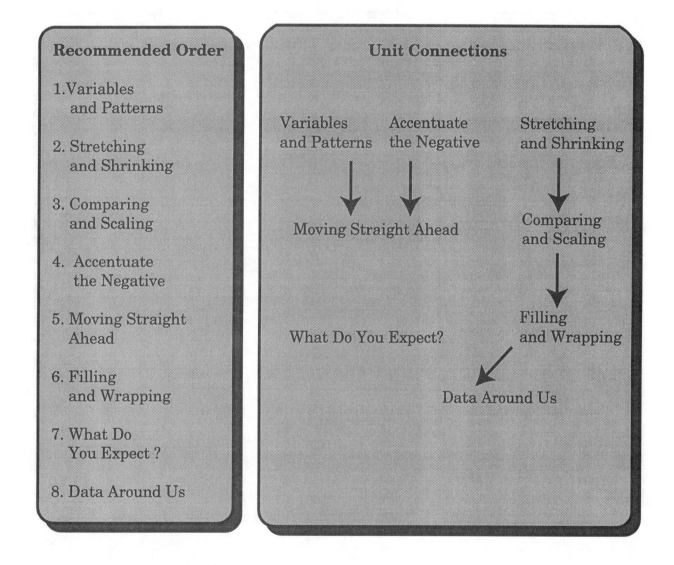

Recommended Order

1. Variables and Patterns

2. Stretching and Shrinking

3. Comparing and Scaling

4. Accentuate the Negative

5. Moving Straight Ahead

6. Filling and Wrapping

7. What Do You Expect?

8. Data Around Us

Unit Connections

Variables and Patterns → Moving Straight Ahead

Accentuate the Negative → Moving Straight Ahead

Stretching and Shrinking → Comparing and Scaling → Filling and Wrapping → Data Around Us

What Do You Expect?

Grade 8

Recommended Order

1. Thinking with Mathematical Models

2. Looking for Pythagoras

3. Growing, Growing, Growing...

4. Frogs, Fleas, and Painted Cubes

5. Say It with Symbols

6. Hubcaps, Kaleidoscopes, and Mirrors!

7. Samples and Populations

8. Clever Counting

Unit Connections

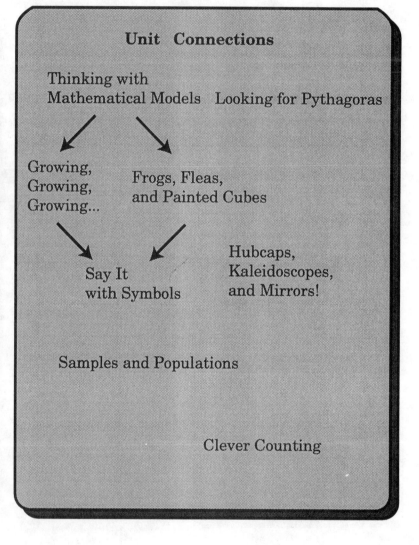

Thinking with Mathematical Models   Looking for Pythagoras

Growing, Growing, Growing...   Frogs, Fleas, and Painted Cubes

Say It with Symbols   Hubcaps, Kaleidoscopes, and Mirrors!

Samples and Populations

Clever Counting

An Overview of the Math Strands in the *CMP* Curriculum

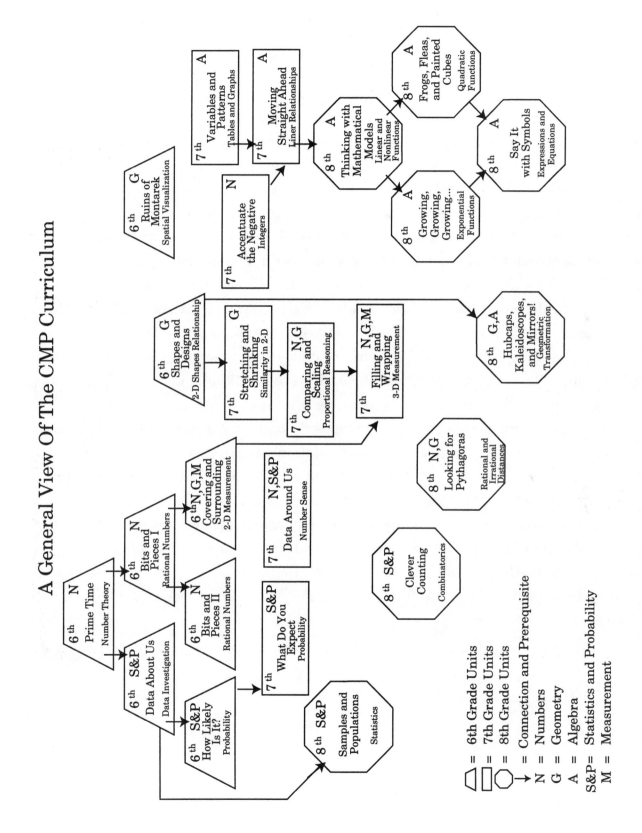

A General View Of The CMP Curriculum

6th Ruins of Montarek — G — Spatial Visualization

7th Variables and Patterns — A — Tables and Graphs

7th Moving Straight Ahead — A — Linear Relationships

7th Accentuate the Negative — N — Integers

8th Thinking with Mathematical Models — A — Linear and Nonlinear Functions

8th Frogs, Fleas, and Painted Cubes — A — Quadratic Functions

8th Growing, Growing, Growing... — A — Exponential Functions

8th Say It with Symbols — A — Expressions and Equations

6th Shapes and Designs — G — 2-D Shapes Relationship

7th Stretching and Shrinking — G — Similarity in 2-D

7th Comparing and Scaling — N, G — Proportional Reasoning

7th Filling and Wrapping — N, G, M — 3-D Measurement

8th Hubcaps, Kaleidoscopes, and Mirrors! — G, A — Geometric Transformation

8th Looking for Pythagoras — N, G — Rational and Irrational Distances

6th Prime Time — N — Number Theory

6th Bits and Pieces I — N — Rational Numbers

6th Covering and Surrounding — N, G, M — 2-D Measurement

6th Bits and Pieces II — N — Rational Numbers

7th Data Around Us — N, S&P — Number Sense

6th Data About Us — S&P — Data Investigation

7th What Do You Expect — S&P — Probability

6th How Likely Is It? — S&P — Probability

8th Samples and Populations — S&P — Statistics

8th Clever Counting — S&P — Combinatorics

Legend

- ⬡ ⬡ ⬣ → = 6th Grade Units
- = 7th Grade Units
- = 8th Grade Units
- → = Connection and Prerequisite
- N = Numbers
- G = Geometry
- A = Algebra
- S&P = Statistics and Probability
- M = Measurement

ALGEBRA IN *CMP*

Many people think of algebra as a course at high school, towards which all prior mathematics has been heading. Students enter the traditional course somewhat in awe of the lofty position they have reached, and are often discouraged to find that the mathematical ideas and skills they have previously developed do not seem related to success in a traditional Algebra 1. The popular impression in the community at large is that algebra is the ability to manipulate symbols, usually following instructions to "simplify" an expression, or "solve" an equation. Traditionally students memorize rules, focusing on specific strategies for specific problems. The symbols and rules often are meaningless to students, who try to survive by memorizing and, thus, only retain the ideas for a short time. There is little evidence that students develop algebraic reasoning, including symbolic reasoning, from this kind of experience. In fact, the development of algebraic ideas can and should take place over a long period of time, prior to attempts to deal solely with abstract symbols, and well before the first year of high school. The development of algebra in the *CMP* curriculum is consistent with *CMP*'s underlying philosophy of how students learn mathematics—that is, students develop algebraic reasoning and understanding while pursuing solutions to interesting problems.

Having students approach algebraic ideas through investigations and problems allows students to search for patterns and relationships in data, and to find ways to express these patterns, first in words and then in symbols. The algebraic units in *CMP* develop three important patterns, which model many real situations. By focusing on the patterns underlying the problem, asking students to describe similarities and differences across patterns, and challenging students to predict answers, the mathematics of functions and relationships is developed. For example, in the Walkathon Problem, in the unit entitled *Moving Straight Ahead,* students investigate the distance each person walks.

2.3 Walkathon

Your class decides to raise money for a charity by competing in the city's Walkathon. Each person in the class finds sponsors who each pledge to pay a certain amount of money for each kilometer that the person walks. The money goes to a charity. The person who raises the most money receives a new pair of Rollerblades™. Sponsors often ask for a suggestion of how much they should pay per kilometer. Others will follow the example of the first person who fills out the form. Your class would like to agree on how much money to ask the sponsors for.

Jane argues that one dollar per kilometer would be appropriate. Bill argues for two dollars a kilometer because it would bring in more money. Amy suggested that if the price was too high not as many people would be sponsors—so she suggested that each sponsor pay a $5 donation plus an extra 50 cents per kilometer.

For each price suggestion made by Bill, Jane and Amy,

- Make a table showing the total amount of money a sponsor pays for distances between 1 and 10 miles. This is called a pay plan.
- Sketch a graph of the amount of money a sponsor would pay under each pay plan. Display all the graphs on the same set of axes.
- Write an equation for each of the pay plans which shows how the amount of money a sponsor owes can be calculated from the total distance that a student walked.

a) As the amount of money charged per mile is increased, what effect does this have on the table? On the equation? On the graph?

b) A student walked 8 miles in the Walkathon. How much would her sponsors pay under each of the pay plans? Explain how you arrived at your answers.

c) One of the sponsors paid $10 after the race. How many miles would that sponsor's student have walked under each of the three pay plans? Explain how you arrived at your answers.

d) How is Amy's fixed $5 cost represented in the table? In the equation? In the graph?

In this situation the focus quickly centers on the relationship between the variables. If the rate at which a person walks is fixed, then distance depends upon (or is a function of the) time; that is, distance = rate x time. As students reason about this situation they are encouraged to used *multiple representations*, which help them to show their reasoning and also to develop understanding of the important linear relationship underlying this situation. As the time changes by one unit, the distance changes by a constant amount. This is the key feature of recognizing a linear relationship. By examining and recognizing this constant rate of change in various representations, students develop a deep understanding of the basic linear pattern. The rate at which a person walks is the constant rate of change (or the slope of a straight line). This pattern shows up as a straight line in a graph, as an equation of the form, $y = ax$, and as increments of change in a table. The rate is indicated by the steepness of the line, the coefficient, a, of x in the equation, and the constant increment of change in the table.

A variation of the problem has two brothers involved in a walking race with the younger brother getting a head start. This leads to the equation, $y = ax + b$; where a is the rate at which the younger brother walks and b represents the amount of the head start. Once students have a beginning understanding of linear patterns, they then need help in recognizing this pattern in many different disguises. For example, the cost, C, of buying N compact discs at $15 each is $C = 15N$. Having recognized that this is the same pattern as that in Walkathon problem, students are quickly able to reason about the relationship between the variables.

Using problem situations and multiple representations to represent these situations gives rise to solving equations. For example, students can use tables or graphs or they can reason about the problem. Once students have a good sense of what it means to solve and how these solutions relate to the variables and the problem, then the techniques of solving a linear equation symbolically are developed.

CMP Algebra Goals – by the End of Eighth Grade in *CMP* Most Students Should be Able to:

- Recognize situations in which important problems and decisions involve relations among quantitative variables—one variable changing over time or several variables changing in response to each other.
- Use numerical tables, graphs, symbolic expressions, and verbal descriptions to describe and predict the patterns of change in variables.

- Recognize (in various representational forms) the patterns of change associated with linear, exponential, and quadratic functions.
- Use numeric, graphic, and symbolic strategies to solve common problems involving linear, exponential, and quadratic functions.

Inevitably parents and teachers will wonder how the *CMP* algebra strand relates to and can be compared to a traditional school algebra curriculum. The only helpful comparison to make is how well students understand algebraic ideas, and how well they employ algebraic reasoning in solving problems. Since the focus of *CMP* is on developing understanding, rather than on memorizing rules and processes to apply in response to instructions such as "simplify" or "solve," a simple checklist of concepts or skills that appear in *CMP* and in traditional programs is not particularly relevant. The question of most interest to parents and teachers should be, "How well will the next mathematics course my student takes support the strong understanding of algebraic ideas developed in *CMP*?" If the next course is a traditional Algebra 1, *CMP* students will find themselves spending large amounts of time studying processes and rules for which they see no application. The motivation for learning these rules may shift from the focus of "making sense" to simply memorizing to survive. Certainly *CMP* students will find that many of the big ideas in Algebra 1, such as representing linear functions, solving equations, and finding equivalent forms of an expression, are familiar, and perhaps a repetition of what they already know. They will also wonder why the problems are restricted mainly to linear patterns, whereas in *CMP* they had also learned about other important patterns. The algebra strand in *CMP* will certainly prepare students for a successful, if somewhat repetitive, year in a traditional Algebra 1. It is to be hoped, however, that students will be fortunate enough to find themselves able to take courses that continue to challenge them to develop algebraic reasoning. High school teachers of these students need to be aware that these students have begun to develop an understanding of functions that is far beyond a traditional Algebra 1 approach.

What the Traditional Curricula (Algebra 1) Include that *CMP* Does Not

- Emphasis on manipulating symbolic expressions, such as multiplying and factoring polynomials.
- Operations on algebraic fractions.
- Formal solutions of linear systems in 2 or more variables.
- Formal study of direct and inverse variation.
- Radicals and simplifications of radicals.
- Operations on polynomials other than linear polynomials.
- Completion of the square and the quadratic formula.

What *CMP* Curriculum Includes that the Traditional Curricula Do Not

- Emphasis on variables and the representations of the relation between variables in words, numeric tables, graphs and symbolic statements.
- Focus, on the rate of change between two variables, not only linear.
- Development of functional point of view and applications.
- Emphasis on modeling
- Earlier introduction of exponential growth and decay
- Development of alternative strategies for answering questions about algebraic expressions and equations, e.g., tables and graphing calculators)

THE ROLE OF TECHNOLOGY IN *CMP*

The content and design of the *CMP* curriculum reflects two central assumptions about electronic technology: (1) Students will have access to calculators at all times—in the 6th Grade students need standard, four-function calculators; in the 7th and 8th Grades we assume that students will have graphing calculators with table and statistical-display capability; and, (2) computer software will be provided with the curriculum that students will be able to use in tandem with the curriculum.

As an example of how technology is used in the *CMP* curriculum, a description of a piece of software for the 6th Grade unit *How Likely Is It?* is included below.

Investigation 1 of *How Likely Is It?* includes a problem about a boy who always wants to eat "Cocoablast" cereal for breakfast, while his mother wants him to eat "Health Nut Flakes." To determine which cereal he will eat, he and his mother decide that he should flip a coin each morning. If the coin lands on heads, he gets to eat Cocoablast. Students flip coins for each day of a month, record percent of heads on a day-to-day basis, then graph the percent of heads versus number of days.

As data is collected from the trials in a classroom, students will begin to make sense of the Law of Large Numbers. Most students know that a fair coin can be expected to land heads about half the time. As they observe the results of their group's 30 flips, and the results of other groups, they may see quite a lot of variation in the percent of heads. However, when the data of the entire class is combined, the total percent of heads will likely be quite close to 50%. Thus, students begin to understand that a larger number of trials will produce results closer to the theoretical probability.

At this point, teachers may choose to introduce the *Coin Game*, a computer program that simulates flipping a coin. If the "fair coin" option is chosen, the computer will randomly generate numbers in two value ranges. This models flipping a coin with a probability of heads equal to 50%. Percent of heads is then graphed on the computer screen in the same way the students manually graphed their data.

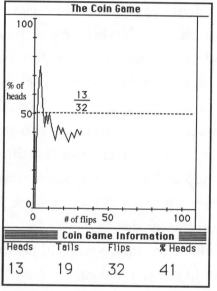

This program allows students, in less than a minute, to "flip," record, and graph the results of up to 10,000 coin tosses. As students experiment with large sets of data, they begin to understand subtle points about the Law of Large Numbers, and the more general concept of convergence to a limit, that may be otherwise inaccessible.

Students often have misconceptions about probability. For example, many students assume (incorrectly) that the Law of Large Numbers means that, if the number of flips is some high number, then *exactly* 50% of the flips will be heads. If students are restricted to flipping coins themselves, they may not have a body of evidence that will convince them otherwise. However, as they use this computer program, students will encounter a variety of situations that may challenge them to rethink their ideas. They might observe, after a moderate number of flips, that the percent of heads reaches 50%, then perhaps moves up to 51%, then perhaps back down to 50%. Additionally, they may see examples of the numbers of heads and tails being close, as in the picture above (only six more tails than heads), after a small number of flips. Then, after 1,000 or more flips, the *difference* between the number of heads and the number of tails might have *increased*, while the *percent* of heads has gotten closer to 50%.

The computer also maintains a record of the results of each flip, so students may, at any time, see the results of the last few flips. This will help students see that a small selection of random flips does not have a predictable pattern, whether it happens to be the first ten flips or flips 5,001 through 5,010. The computer provides a concrete experience with a sophisticated idea.

We do not suggest that this software is absolutely essential for students to learn a great deal about probability. However, for many students, using the computer will broaden their understanding of the mathematics in the *How Likely Is It?* unit. In general, that is how we have designed all the computer and graphing calculator activities in this curriculum. Technology has been embedded in ways that allow students to have a richer mathematical experience.

Because we use computer and graphing calculator activities quite selectively, there will not be an electronic technology component in each unit. About half the 6th Grade units have computer activities. Seventh and 8th Grade units include generally a bit less computer work, but roughly half the units do include graphing calculator activities.

While most classrooms will be able to supply calculators, we realize that availability of computers will vary. Many configurations are possible. The optimal computer environments are either several computers within the mathematics classroom, or regular access by the mathematics class to a computer laboratory. Some activities, such as the *Coin Game* described above, can also enhance the curriculum when used in a classroom with a single computer equipped with an overhead display. There are also a few activities, such as the computer *Factor Game* from the *Prime Time* unit, which lend themselves to enrichment work. Typically, this software may be installed on a single computer to which students have intermittent access.

Whatever the computer configuration, we feel it is worthwhile to make the effort to bring technology into the classroom. There are some mathematics concepts that naturally lend themselves to exploration with computer and calculator technology. Additionally, computers and calculators can play an important part in addressing the wide range of learning styles within the classroom.

II. Student Materials:

STRUCTURE AND ORGANIZATION OF THE STUDENT MATERIALS IN *CMP*

In a broad sense, observations of regularity in patterns and relationships lie at the heart of acquiring understanding in mathematics. Therefore, the curriculum is organized around rich problem settings—real situations, whimsical situations, or interesting mathematical situations. Students solve problems and in so doing they observe patterns and relationships; they conjecture, test, discuss, verbalize, and generalize these patterns and relationships. Through this process they discover the salient features of the pattern or relationship; construct understandings of concepts, processes, and relationships; develop a language to talk about the problem; and learn to integrate and discriminate among patterns or relationships. The students engage in making sense of the problems that are posed, and with the aide of the teacher, to abstract powerful mathematical ideas, problem solving strategies, and ways of thinking that are made accessible by the investigations.

FEATURES OF STUDENT MATERIALS

The curriculum is organized into units that investigate important mathematical ideas. An outline of the features of a unit is given and then a discussion of each feature follows:

Features of a Unit
- A set of **Focusing Questions to Think About** to pique student curiosity about what they will learn in the unit.
- **Mathematical Highlight**s of the unit listed as goals for students.
- Some units have a final **Project** that is launched at the beginning of the unit.
- Four to Seven **Investigations** each of which has the following features:
  - ✔ A short discussion to set the theme for the investigation.
  - ✔ One to four **Problems** are posed to be discussed and solved over several days.
  - ✔ Homework is assigned regularly from the **Applications – Connections – Extensions** Section.
  - ✔ The investigation is summarized with a **Mathematical Reflections** section.

Focusing Questions

Each unit is organized around a cluster of concepts that are related to the mathematical goals. The mathematical theme of this cluster of concepts is set at the beginning of each unit through some interesting problems or issues for students to **Think About.** These focusing problems are not solved in the beginning of the unit, but are returned to at the point in the unit when the students have developed some ideas and strategies that make the problems accessible. These problems are seen as a way to draw the students into the unit, to pique their curiosity and point the way to the kinds of ideas that the unit will investigate.

Example of **Focus Questions:** *Covering and Surrounding*—Grade 6.

- Pizza parlors often describe their selections as 9-inch, 12-inch, 15-inch, or even 24-inch pizzas. What do these measurements tell you about pizza size? How does the size of a pizza relate to its price? Does a 24-inch pizza generally cost twice as much as a 12-inch pizza? Should price relate to the size in that way?

- Carpet is commonly sold by the square yard. How would you estimate the cost of carpet for a room in your home? Base molding, which is used to protect the basses of walls, is usually sold by the foot. How would you estimate the cost of base molding for a room in your home?

- You may know that China has the greatest population of any country. Which country do you think has the greatest land area? The longest borders? Which state in the United States is the largest? Which state is the smallest? How do you think land area, borders, and coastlines of sates and countries are measure?

Mathematical Highlights

Each unit has a set of goals (**Mathematical Highlights**) that represent the big ideas in the unit. These goals are written to help the students see their own progress through the unit. They are also ways for parents and guardians to see what mathematical concepts, processes, and mathematical ways of thinking the unit will help students develop. This set of goals points the student to what the teacher expects the students to learn and is reflected in the suggested assessment tasks.

Example of **Mathematical Highlights** from *Covering and Surrounding*—
Grade 6.

Mathematical Highlights

In *Covering and Surrounding*, you will learn about area and perimeter.

- Designing and comparing floor plans for bumper-car rides helps you understand perimeter and area.
- Tracing and measuring your foot helps you develop ways to reason about the perimeter and area of odd shapes.
- Designing different storm shelters with the same area illustrates how perimeters of figures with the same area can vary.
- Investigating the different dog pens you can build with a fixed amount of fencing shows you how the area of figures with the same perimeter can vary.
- Measuring parallelograms drawn on grid paper, building parallelograms under constraints, and making a rectangle by cutting apart a parallelogram and reassembling it lead you to discover shortcuts for finding the area and perimeter of a parallelogram.
- Measuring triangles drawn on grid paper, building triangles under constraints, and making parallelograms from two copies of a triangle lead you to discover a shortcut for finding the area of a triangle.
- Finding area and circumferences of pizzas and other circular objects helps you find patterns relating the radius and diameter to the area and the circumference.
- Covering a circle with "radius squares" leads you to discover the formula for the area of a circle.

Investigations

Each unit is developed around a series of four to seven **Investigations**. Each investigation has one to four related **Problems** for the students to solve, a set of questions for homework—applications, connecting and extension; and a mathematical reflection. The length of an investigation varies depending on how much time is needed to develop the mathematical ideas.

Problems with Follow-Up

A problem from an investigation may take more than a class period depending on the length of the period and the challenge of the problem. The problems are designed to allow students to bump into the mathematics that is embedded in the situation as they work in pairs or groups to solve the problems. The teacher is expected to pull the class together at the end of each problem and at the end of a whole investigation to help the students explicitly describe the mathematical ideas, patterns and relationships and the strategies that they found and used in the investigation. *The teacher plays a central role in making the mathematics come alive.*

Example of a **Problem** from the *Covering and Surrounding*—Grade 6.

Problem 7.1: The Sole D'Italia Pizzeria sells small, medium, and large pizzas. A small is 9 inches in diameter, a medium is 12 inches in diameter, and a large is 15 inches in diameter. Prices for cheese pizzas are $6.00 for small, $9.00 for medium, and $12.00 for large.

a) Draw a 9-inch, 12-inch, and a 15-inch "pizza" on centimeter grid paper. Let 1 centimeter of the grid paper represent 1 inch on the pizza. Estimate the radius, circumference, and area of each pizza. (You may want to use string to help you find the circumference.)

b) Which measurement—radius, diameter, circumference, or area—seems most closely related to price? Explain your answer.

Problem 7.1 Follow-Up

Use your results to write a report about what you consider to be the best value of the pizza options at Sole D'Italia.

Applications – Connections – Extensions

Each investigation is accompanied by a set of problems that can be used for homework or extensions to keep all students engaged in pushing further what they

---

know about the area of mathematics under investigation. These problems are organized around three headings—**Applications – Connections – Extensions (ACE)**.

Applications

In the **Applications** section the problems help examine the mathematics and the strategies developed in each problem of the investigation, in contexts both similar and different from those used in the investigation problems. This section is meant to provide practice with the ideas and to help students cement their understanding of the ideas and concepts. This might be thought of as developing both understanding and skill in using the ideas of the investigation. The ACE part of each investigation is an important step in the process of developing students' understanding of the big mathematical ideas and processes.

Example of **Application** problems from *Covering and Surrounding*—Grade 6.

---

4. If the spray from a lawn sprinkler makes a circle 40 feet in radius, what are the approximate diameter, circumference, and area of the circle of lawn watered?
5. A standard long-playing record album has a 12-inch diameter; a compact disc has a 5-inch diameter. Find the radius, circumference, and area of each.

Connections

In the **Connections** section, the problems are connected to the new mathematics of the investigation, but are also connected to the other units that have been studied previously. For example, a data unit occurs early in the beginning of Grade 6. Many succeeding units have some problems that explore the new ideas in the context of gathering and organizing data. Thus one goal of the **Connections** sections is to keep the mathematics studied so far alive for the students. As ideas are developed they are then used throughout the remaining units. Other connections help the students see the mathematics that is being studied connected to other school subjects and to the world of the students. Therefore, the connections problems are often set in contexts that come from real world problems or other disciplines.

Example of a **Connection** problem from *Covering and Surrounding*—
Grade 6, that connects to real world uses.

Some everyday circular objects are commonly described by giving their radius or diameter. In 9–12, explain what useful information (if any) you would get from calculating the area or circumference of the circle.

9. a 3.5-inch-diameter computer disk
10. a 21-inch-diameter bicycle wheel
11. a 12-inch-diameter water pipe
12. a lawn sprinkler that sprays a 15-meter-radius section of lawn

Extensions

The final section of the problems is called **Extensions.** Here problems might push the mathematics of the investigation further or deeper. They might call for research or additional reading on the situation underlying one of the investigations. The problems might also extend the mathematics by foreshadowing ideas that are to come. Questions that are accessible to the students through the mathematics of the current investigation, but that also are connected to what is coming up would be of this type. Throughout the ACE problems students are asked to reason, connect, solve problems, and communicate their ideas in writing and orally; in addition, they are asked to compare, visualize, model, measure, count, and use tools.

The following is an example of an **Extension** problem from *Covering and Surrounding*—Grade 6, that pushes students to abstract and generalize what they have learned about the relationship between perimeter and area.

17. Suppose you tie together the ends of a piece of string that is 60 centimeters long.

a) Suppose you arranged the string to form an equilateral triangle. What would the area of the enclosed space be? What would the area be if you formed a square? A regular hexagon?

Think back to the work you did in *Shapes and Designs*. Why do you think the surface of a honeycomb is covered with hexagons?

b) Of all the rectangles with a perimeter of 60 centimeters, which has greatest area?

c) Of all the triangles with a perimeter of 60 centimeters, which has greatest area?

d) How does the area of a regular octagon with a perimeter of 60 centimeters compare to the areas of a triangle, a square, and a hexagon with perimeters of 60 centimeters?

e) What happens to the enclosed area as the 60-centimeter perimeter is used to make regular polygons or more and more sides? (If you have access to a computer and the Logo programming language, you might use the computer to draw these figures.)

f) As the number of sides of a polygon gets larger and larger, what shape does the polygon eventually resemble?

One caveat is in order. The classification of a problem as an application, a connection, or an extension is not definitive. Some problem are so rich that they could be classified in two or more ways. We have used the classifications to help you and the students keep these three important aspects of learning mathematics constantly in focus. To truly own an idea, strategy, or concept, a student has to apply/use it, connect it to what they already know or have experienced, and seek ways to extend or generalize it. It is in this spirit of learning mathematics that we have labeled sections of the homework ACE. Problems are selected for ACE with an eye to what mathematics can be supported through the problem and how useful or applicable this mathematics is. A problem may be included in the ACE section because the problem solving methods, the ways of reasoning, or even the ways of organizing data and evidence to support conjectures in the problem are of great use in mathematics.

Reflections

The students write about their work on a regular basis. As Britton wrote in 1970 in *Language and Learning,*

> *...Speaking and writing are commentary or a way of making sense out of our random perceptions. We must write or speak about an experience to make sense of it...*

In addition to the writing embedded in the problems, at the end of each investigation students are asked to reflect on what they have learned. The materials include a set of organizing questions, a *CMP* feature called **Mathematical Reflections**, to help students summarize the big ideas in the investigation. After sketching out their own ideas, the students discuss the questions with their teacher and classmates, and then write their own summary of the "big ideas." This section occurs at the end of each investigation and is meant to be used by the students and the teacher after the students have completed the investigation problems and the Applications – Connections – Extensions section.

Example of a **Mathematical Reflection** from *Covering and Surrounding—* Grade 6. Notice that this asks for a written record of the students' ideas in their journals.

Mathematical Reflections
Investigation Seven

In this investigation, you discovered strategies for finding the area and circumference (perimeter) of a circle. You examined relationships between the circumference and the diameter of a circle and between the area and the radius of a circle. These questions will help you summarize what you have learned.

1. Describe how you can find the circumference of a circle by measuring the radius or the diameter. If you need to, explain your thinking by using a specific circle.

2. Describe how you can find the area of a circle by measuring its radius or its diameter. If you need to, explain your thinking by using a specific circle. Why is your method useful?

    Think about your answers to these questions, discuss your ideas with other students and your teacher, and then write a summary of your findings in your journal.
    You will soon be designing your layout for the city park. How might your new information about circles help you? What objects in your park might be in the shape of a circle—a flower garden, a water fountain?

Project

Some of the units have a project. Covering and Surrounding has a project that is described on page 57.

III. Teaching the *CMP* Curriculum:

PROBLEM-CENTERED TEACHING
THE FOCUS OF *CMP* TEACHING AND LEARNING

The NCTM *Professional Standards for Teaching* gives a vision of the teaching needed to realize the goal of mathematical power for all students. The *Standards* that put forward this vision are organized around four aspects of teaching that are judged to be so central to good teaching that they provide us with a framework for decision making. These four aspects of decision making are choosing *worthwhile mathematical tasks*, orchestrating classroom *discourse*, creating an *environment* for learning, and *analyzing* teaching and learning. In *CMP* we have tried to provide teachers with ways to think about and try in their classroom problem–centered teaching that pays attention to these four aspects of teaching.

WORTHWHILE MATHEMATICAL TASKS

There is no other decision that teachers make that has a greater impact on students' opportunity to learn and on their perceptions about what mathematics is than the selection or creation of the tasks with which the teacher engages the students in studying mathematics. To develop more productive notions about mathematics, students must have opportunities to actually be involved in doing mathematics—to explore interesting mathematical situations, to look for patterns, to make conjectures, to look for evidence to support their conjectures, to make logical arguments for their conjectures.

What is a good task? In *CMP* we have said that a good task is one that supports some or all the following:

- Students can approach the problem in multiple ways using different solution strategies.
- The problem has important, useful mathematics embedded in it.
- The problem may have different solutions or may allow different decisions or positions to be taken and defended.
- The problem encourages student engagement and discourse.
- The problem requires higher level thinking and problem solving.
- The problem contributes to the conceptual development of students.
- The problem promotes the skillful use of mathematics.

- The problem can create an opportunity for the teacher to assess what his or her students are learning and where they are having difficulty.

We believe that problems should not be chosen just because they are "fun," or use a manipulative that is available in the classroom. There must be the potential for students to engage in sound and significant mathematics as a part of accomplishing the task. But a teacher teaches particular students, and their needs or interests must be taken into account. Therefore a teacher using *CMP* is encouraged to choose an alternative setting for a problem if his or her students are likely to find the alternative setting more engaging. What the students already know and can do, what their mathematical needs are and the level of challenge they seem ready to accept are all fundamental issues for a teacher. Therefore, we encourage teachers to use their professional judgment to help students succeed in *CMP*.

Classroom Discourse

The *Professional Standards for Teaching Mathematics (PSTM)* describes discourse as "the ways of representing, thinking, talking, agreeing, and disagreeing" (1991, p. 36) as a group of students and a teacher strive to make sense of mathematics. Discourse includes the ways that ideas are represented, exchanged, and modified into more powerful and useful ideas. Teachers have a critical role to play in establishing the norms of discourse in the classroom and orchestrating discourse on a daily basis. It is through the interactions in the classroom that students learn what mathematical activities are acceptable, which need to be explained or justified, and what explanations or justifications are acceptable.

The *CMP* materials, for both student and teacher, are designed in ways that help students and teachers build a different pattern of interaction in the classroom. The *CMP* materials try to support a teacher and students in building a community of learners that are mutually supportive as they work together to make sense of the mathematics. We do this through the tasks that are provided, the justification that students are asked to provide on a regular basis, the opportunities to talk about and write about their ideas, and the help for the teacher in both alternative forms of assessment and using a problem–centered instructional model in the classroom. We will talk about this model for instruction and assessment in later sections of this booklet.

Environment

What students learn is fundamentally connected to how they learn it. The environment in which students learn affects their views of what mathematics is, how one learns it, and perhaps of more importance, their views of themselves as learners of mathematics. Environment means more than the physical surroundings. It includes the messages that students are given about what is expected of them. What is their work to be? What counts in the classroom? Is it speed? Neatness? Being quiet? Completing tasks? Or is it taking responsibility for listening to and helping others? Asking questions of themselves and of their classmates? Seeking evidence? Being curious? Working independently? Sharing ideas and strategies?

Environment encompasses considerations of tasks and discourse and the emotional climate of the classroom. Is the environment of the classroom conducive to taking intellectual risks? Does every student feel valued? Does every student feel that their ideas will be respected even if they turn out to be incorrect? Does every student expect to make conjectures or argue points or question each other as they build their mathematical understanding?

The Mathematical Sciences Education Board, in a Background Paper for its National Summit on Mathematics Assessment, talks about environments that are supportive of the vision of mathematical power for all students as environments that do the following:

- encourage students to explore;
- help students verbalize their mathematical ideas;
- show students that many mathematical questions have more than one right answer;
- teach through experience the importance of careful reasoning and disciplined understanding; and
- build confidence in all children that they can learn mathematics.

CMP supports the creation of this kind of environment for learning mathematics. In the teacher materials, ideas from the many teachers that have used *CMP* during the trials are included to give ideas about how to begin to establish an environment that supports students taking more responsibility for making sense of mathematics. *Change is hard. Students may not like mathematics, yet may still resist any attempts of the teacher to change the culture of the classroom.* Students may be used to a mathematics classroom where little is required of them beyond practicing the idea that was illustrated by the teacher in the first part of the lesson. *CMP* teachers have found that perseverance works. Students, resistant in September, are fully engaged by January. We are also finding that the second year in *CMP*, students start the year expecting to tackle more challenging problems and to construct arguments to justify their thinking and reasoning. They understand the demands of working in pairs, in groups, and individually. Establishing the expectation and pattern of classroom discourse is much easier.

Analysis

How well is the classroom working? Are the tasks engaging the students? Are they effective in helping students learn mathematics? Do they stimulate the richness of discussion that students need to develop mathematical power? Is the classroom discourse fostering learner independence? Curiosity? Mathematical thinking? Confidence? Disposition to do mathematics? Is the classroom environment encouraging the kind of engagement that reaches every student and supports their mathematical development? These are the kinds of questions that reflective teachers regularly ask themselves. The teaching standards refers to these aspects of teacher reflection as analysis. Analysis also includes the regular assessment of student progress for the purpose of making instructional decisions. In other words, what do my students know? What is my evidence? How does this shape what I plan for tomorrow? This broad view of analysis is supportive of the concern in the *Curriculum Standards* for the mathematical development of children to include learning to value mathematics, to have confidence in themselves as learners of mathematics, and to be able to use mathematics to solve problems. This clearly calls for the teacher to look carefully at the complex set of activities and interaction in the classroom with an eye on whether and how students are learning. The assessment tasks that *CMP* provides, and the examples of student work and teacher commentary included in the teacher material, are all meant to help a teacher analyze what his or her students are learning both for reporting grades and for making instructional decisions. In the next section we take a closer look at the structure of the teacher materials for *CMP*.

STRUCTURE OF TEACHER MATERIALS IN THE *CONNECTED MATHEMATICS PROJECT*

Extensive try-outs of the *CMP* curriculum have helped to produce teacher materials that are rich with examples of successful strategies that trial teachers used, classroom dialogues and questions, and student responses. The teacher materials contain a discussion of the mathematics underlying the investigations in a unit and the mathematical and problem solving goals for the unit. A list of the materials needed, suggested time-lines for teaching, homework assignment choices, and an essential vocabulary list are given for each unit. In addition, the teacher materials contain a student assessment package, often including a suggested project, that a teacher can use or alter to fit his or her situation. Black line masters of needed consumable student pages and black line masters for overhead transparencies for teaching are included.

In the teachers' edition a list of vocabulary items is included to help the teacher and the students focus on what may be new language for the students. Among the list of vocabulary words are some that are marked as *essential*. What distinguishes these words from the others on the list is the breadth of their use in mathematics. In marking a work essential, a judgment is made that this word represents a concept that is useful in many mathematical situations. For example, the word "prime" is essential because many mathematical problems and situations are better understood and solved by looking at the prime structure of numbers. However, knowing the word "abundant" for numbers, the sum of proper factors that exceeds the number, is interesting, but not likely to occur in many mathematical situations other than number theory. We use abundant in the unit, but do not mark it as essential because it is of local, not global, interest and use in mathematics.

The intent of the teacher material is to make the teaching of *CMP* as smooth as possible the first year that a teacher tries the material. We recognize that as teachers become more experienced with *CMP*, they begin to find their own "personality" and what works for their students in this new kind of teaching. To help teachers survive and want to teach *CMP* again, the materials include the following:

Overview of Unit
- Big mathematical ideas of unit and investigations
- Mathematical and problem solving goals
- Material and time-lines for the unit

Teaching Notes for Each Investigation

- A problem by problem discussion with examples of the instructional roles of the teacher during all phases of the lessons:

  Launch – Explore – Summarize

- Convenient outline of key points in Launch – Explore – Summarize Phases
- Appropriate ACE Assignment
- Sample of Student Responses to Questions
- Complete Solutions to Investigations and ACE Questions

Assessment Items

- Partner Quizzes
- Check–ups
- Projects
- Unit Tests
- Self–Assessment
- Question Bank

Appendices

- Students' Work and Scoring Suggestions, or Teaching and Management Stereotypes or Vignettes
- Blackline Masters
- Transparencies, and Consumable Student Labsheets
- Parent Letter

Descriptive Glossary/Index

THE *CMP* INSTRUCTIONAL MODEL

Problem–centered teaching, which opens the mathematics classroom to exploring, conjecturing, reasoning, and communicating, requires a different instructional model than the "transmission" model of mathematics teaching in which teachers tell students facts and demonstrate procedures and the students memorize the facts and practice the procedures. The *CMP* teacher materials are organized around an instructional model that supports problem–centered teaching. This model looks at instruction in three phases—*launching, exploring, and summarizing.*

Launch

During the first phase, the teacher *launches* the investigation with the whole class by setting the context for the problem. This involves making sure that the students understand the setting or situation in which the problem is posed. But of more importance is being sure that the problem is launched in such a way that the mathematical context and mathematical challenge is clear. What are students expected to do? How are they expected to record and report their work? Will they be in pairs or groups? Will they be expected to think about the problem individually before working with their partners or group members? What tools are available that might be helpful? This is also the time when, if necessary, the teacher introduces new ideas, clarifies definitions, reviews old concepts, and connects this problem to past experiences of the students. One thing that teachers need to monitor is whether they are launching tasks in such a way that the potential of the task is left intact even though students are given a clear picture of what is expected. It is easy to tell too much and lower the challenge of the task to something that is fairly routine.

Example of Discussion of **Launching** a Problem for *Covering and Surrounding*—Grade 6.

Launch

This problem asks students to think about how a pizza is priced relative to its diameter, radius, circumference, and area. Students are asked to find these measures for three different circular pizzas and to decide which measures are most closely related to price. The purpose of the problem is to encourage students to think about measuring circles, not to introduce formulas. We envision them using counting and estimating strategies to find area and circumference. Problems 7.2–7.4 will help them discover the formulas for the circumference and area of a circle.

Discuss the ideas presented in the overview of the investigation in the student edition. Make sure students understand what the diameter, radius, and circumference of a circle are.

Read Problem 7.1 with the class. It would be helpful to have models of the three pizzas (cut from transparent grid paper) as you review the questions posed in the problem. Discuss how students can use a compass to make their own models by drawing circles on centimeter grid paper using a 1 inch = 1 centimeter scale. If they have trouble with this scaled model, let them use large sheets of inch grid paper or tape together several sheets to make circles the actual size of the pizzas.

Students are asked to find several pieces of data to help them answer the questions. Remind them to organize the information they collect so they can look for patterns and make comparisons more easily.

Explore

The second phase, *exploration,* is the time for students to work in pairs, in small groups or individually (or sometimes as a whole class) to solve the problem by gathering data, sharing ideas, looking for patterns, making conjectures, or developing other types of problem-solving strategies. It is inevitable that students will exhibit variation in their progress. The teacher's role during the exploration is to move about the classroom, observing individual performances and encouraging on-task behavior. The teacher urges students to persevere in seeking a solution to the challenge by asking appropriate questions and by providing confirmation and redirection where needed. For more able and more interested students, the teacher provides extra challenges related to the ideas embedded in the problem.

Example of Discussion of **Exploring** a Problem for *Covering and Surrounding*—Grade 6.

Explore

Have students work in pairs or small groups to find the radius, circumference, and area of each circle. As you visit the groups, make sure they are recording their findings and can explain how they arrived at their answers. After students have completed the problem, have them write the report suggested in the follow-up.

Summarize

The final phase of instruction, *summarizing*, occurs when most of the students have gathered sufficient data or made sufficient progress toward solving the problem. Here the teacher helps the class to discuss ways they found to organize the data and to look for patterns and related rules in the data. Discussing the strategies used by students to attack the problem helps the teacher to guide them in refining these strategies into efficient, effective problem-solving techniques. It is during the summarizing phase that the teacher helps students to deepen their understanding of the mathematical ideas involved in the challenge, the strategies used to solve it and the connections to other mathematical ideas and applications. The ultimate goal is for the students to play a larger and larger role in the summary through involvement in the classroom discourse—posing conjectures, questioning each other, offering alternatives, providing reasons, refining their strategies or conjectures, making connections, and becoming more skillful at using the ideas and techniques that come out of the experience with the problem. During the summarizing, content goals can be addressed, allowing the teacher to assess the degree to which students are secure in their mathematical knowledge. This allows further instructional decisions to be made that are in the best interest of the students.

Example of Discussion of **Summarizing** a Problem for *Covering and Surrounding*—Grade 6.

Summarize

On the board or overhead projector, record the measurements that students found for the radius, circumference, and area of each circle. Discuss how they found the measurements and whether any seem unreasonable. Because students are counting and estimating, circumferences and areas will vary, but should be within a reasonable range.

Size	Diameter	Radius	Circumference	Area
small	9 inches	4.5 inches	28.3 inches	63.6 sq. in.
medium	12 inches	6 inches	37.7 inches	113.1 sq. in.
large	15 inches	7.5 inches	47.1 inches	176.7 sq. in.

Since students have found formulas for perimeter and area of several polygons, they may ask what the formulas are for circumference and area of a circle. They may tire of fitting a string and counting squares after just a few examples. Reflect the question back to them.

Do you see any patterns in the measurements that might help you predict circumference and area?

Do not give the formulas now unless students see the relationships among diameter, radius, circumference, and area and can explain why they make sense.

Discuss the answers to part B, and have students present the reports they wrote for the follow-up. Students will probably need help in deciding how to compare the pizzas. Many will say that the diameter is most closely related to price because as it changes by 3 inches, the price changes by $3.00.

GROUPING STUDENTS IN *CMP*

The *Connected Mathematics Project* provides opportunities for students to work on problems individually, in pairs, in small groups, and as a whole class. Deciding when and how to group students is a function of the size and difficulty of a problem, as well as whether you are launching into the problem, exploring the problem in-depth, or summarizing and extending the problem.

Individual Work

In the *CMP* units, students are often asked to work individually on a problem during the launch phase of instruction and during the beginning of the explore phase. Asking students to first think about and try a problem on their own gives them time to sort out their own ideas as well as self-assess what makes sense to them and what they are struggling with.

There are a couple of problems in each unit that are somewhat smaller in mathematical demand and time demand. For these few problems we suggest that students launch into the problem and continue to explore these problem on their own, reaching individual solutions.

The ACE problems that follow each investigation are intended to be primarily individual work done outside class. These give students a chance to practice and make sense of ideas presented in class. Most of these problems are smaller than the problems addressed in the investigations.

Small Group Work

CMP teacher materials suggest that students work in small groups for most of the problems in an investigation. After being introduced to a problem, during the launch phrase of instruction, students are grouped together to work and solve the problems. Most of the problems require students to gather data, consider a variety of ideas, look for patterns, make conjectures, and use problem solving strategies to reach a solution. Working with one or more people allows students to tackle more difficult and complicated problems.

Another time that students are asked to work together is for some of the unit projects. Again, these tend to be large complicated tasks that require more than one person so that more ideas are considered and so that the task can be completed in a reasonable amount of time.

Whole Class Grouping

Students are sometimes asked to think about and discuss, as a whole class, the ideas of a problem during the launch phase of instruction. Yet the most common place for whole class grouping in *CMP* is during the summarizing phase of the lesson. Here groups and individuals share their work. With the direction of the teacher they continue to investigate ideas, strategies, and incomplete thoughts until the mathematics in the investigation is made more explicit. Whole class groupings allow for many ideas to be presented. It also allows for further development of ideas by students pushing at and questioning what is presented.

Managing Cooperative Groups

Cooperative learning is a classroom technique that has students working together to solve common problems. This technique can be a powerful tool for teachers to use during classroom instruction. The *Connected Mathematics Project* suggests two types of cooperative learning groupings throughout its curriculum: partner work and small group work. A suggested grouping for most problems is given in the teachers guide based on the size and type of the mathematical tasks posed to students.

Partner Work in *CMP*

Students working with a partner is one of the simplest of the cooperative learning strategies, yet one of the most powerful. Throughout the *CMP* units the teacher guide suggests that students be paired together to work on a problem or set of problems. Using partner groupings is suggested in the following manner.

- The teacher poses a problem to the class.
- Students are asked to think about the problem for a few minutes on their own.
- Students are paired with another student and given a period of time to discuss and continue to work on the problems.
- The class is brought back together and the partner groups share their results with the rest of the class.

Neal Davidson, at the University of Maryland, calls this strategy Think–Pair–Share.

Pairing students together can be done several ways. Some teachers just have students work with the person who sits next to them. Others have students sitting four to a table and on some days have students work with the person next to them and other days with the person across from them. Finding a way to get students quickly into pairs is important so that valuable class time is not wasted figuring out who will work with whom.

After pairs of students have worked together on a problem and the class is brought back together to discussing the findings, it is not important that all groups share every time. When groups are sharing the teacher should be looking for and asking groups to add to the conversation by contributing ideas not yet presented by any other group or by expanding on any ideas given by another group. What is important, is that over a period of time (say a week) a teacher keeps track of which partner groups are sharing and makes sure that each group shares at some point.

Small Group Work In CMP

Students working in groups of three or four is the other cooperative learning strategy that is suggested in the *CMP* teacher guides. This strategy is used with bigger, more complicated problems that require more work. Using small groupings is suggested in the following manner.

- For the most part, groups should be of mixed ability levels and mixed gender.
- The teacher poses a problem to the class.
- Students are asked to think about the problem for a few minutes on their own.
- Groups are given a period of time to discuss and work on the problem and prepare a response.
- The class is brought back together and the groups share their results with the rest of the class.

Determining groups needs to be done is an efficient manner. Many teachers decide how students will be grouped before class begins so that time is not wasted. Some teachers assign students to a group of four for a whole unit of study.

Some problems that arise in small group arrangements are dominance and non-participation. One way that teachers can deal with this is to require group members to take turns sharing and giving ideas when the group first starts to work on a problem. Some teachers require that a round of group brainstorming/sharing be done twice in the group before the conversation is opened up to any and all ideas.

Another problem that arises is that the same person in a group always shares the findings when called back to whole class discussion. Some teachers handle this by giving each student in a group a number and when sharing time comes the teacher decides which number from a group will do the sharing for that day.

It is important that you clearly communicate your expectations to your students about what should take place during group work. Here are some suggestions that teachers have used to help students learn to work in groups.

1. Move into your groups quickly and get right to work.
2. Read any instructions aloud or recap what the teacher has challenged you to find out in your groups. Be sure that every group member knows what the challenge is.
3. Part of group work is learning to listen to each other. Don't interrupt your classmates. Help make sure that every one's ideas are heard and every one's questions are answered by the group.
4. If you are confused, ask your group to explain. If no one in the group can answer the question, and it is an important question, raise your hand for the teacher to help.
5. If one of your group uses a word or an idea that you do not understand, ask for an explanation. You are responsible for learning all that you can from your group. You are also responsible for contributing to the work of your group. Your attempts to explain to others will help you to understand even better.
6. Everyone in the group should have a chance to talk about their ideas on the problem. Talking out loud about your thinking will help you learn to express your arguments and clarify your ideas.
7. If your group gets stuck, go over what the problem is asking and what you know so far. If this does not give you a new idea, raise your hand for the teacher.
8. As you prepare to share what you have found out, summarize what strategies the groups used to solve the problem, how you thought about the problem, and why you think you are correct. Be sure to look back at the original problem and make sure that your answer or answers make sense.

CMP materials help a teacher to look at what students are learning in several different ways. The next section explains the features of the assessment package provided for each unit.

IV. Assessment:

ASSESSMENT IN *CMP*

Assessment in the *CMP* materials is intended as an extension of the learning process for students as well as an opportunity to check what students can do. For this reason the *CMP* assessment is multidimensional, giving students many ways to demonstrate how they are making sense of the mathematics in the units. It is also our belief that students need to have access to the tools that they use when they engage in mathematics every day, during those times when they are being assessed. The collection of assessment instruments are written under this assumption. This collection of resources includes, but is not limited to: calculators, manipulatives, measurement devices, and any items used for specific units. In addition to assessment instruments, *CMP* offers and make reference to organizational tools to help students in their study of the units.

FEATURES OF THE ASSESSMENT PACKAGE

- Check-Ups
- Partner Quizzes
- Projects
- Unit Tests
- Self-Assessment / "Show What You Know"
- Question Banks

Organizational Tools

- Notebooks
- Journals
- Notebook Check
- Vocabulary Lists

In addition to these items, The ACE sections that accompanies each investigation can be used as homework for individual assessment.

Check-Ups

Check-Ups are offered as individual assessment instruments for a unit. The questions asked tend to be smaller questions and more skill oriented. The nature of these questions provides insight into students' understanding of the baseline mathematical concepts of the unit. Student responses to Check-Ups can help teachers in further instructional planning for the unit.

Example of **Check-Up** question from the *Covering and Surrounding*—Grade 6.

1. The following diagram shows several figures drawn on a grid. Calculate the area and perimeter of each figure.

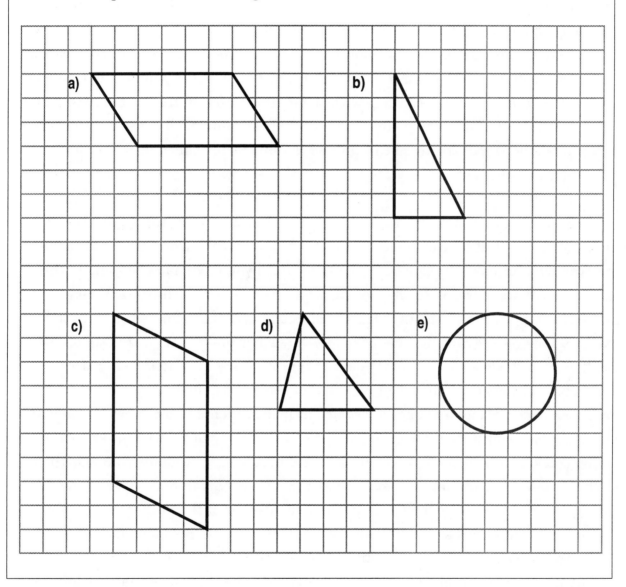

Quizzes

Each unit has a set of Quizzes in its assessment package. Quizzes (sometimes referred to as partner-quizzes) are offered as group assessment. The problems included in the Quizzes are bigger questions, many of which are extensions of the ideas worked on in class. The challenging nature of these questions provides insight into how students use the ideas from the unit in more complicated situations. All quizzes have been written under the following guidelines:

- Students work in pairs on the tasks. (This supports the classroom philosophy of having students work and learn together.) See Appendix C for one teacher's reflections on using partner quizzes.
- Students are able to use their notebooks, calculators, and any other appropriate equipment when doing quizzes.
- Student pairs are given the opportunity to have their quiz examined once by the teacher and they can then revise their work, without penalty. The pair's first attempt at sense-making with the mathematics on the quiz is considered a first draft that is being submitted for teacher input. Following revision based on teacher input the team can turn in the finished product for assessment.

To implement partner-quizzes in classrooms, the teacher or the students pick their partners. Most teachers keep track of who works with whom and have a rule that you can not have the same partner twice until you have had everyone in the class as a partner once. With their partner, students work on the quiz. When the pair has completed the quiz, they turn in one copy, with both names on it, to the teacher. This reduces the number of papers a teacher must read at this time. The teacher gives feedback to a student pair by telling which questions are incorrect or telling how many points they would get out of those possible for a question. Feedback does not mean trying to re-teach or lead students to a correct solution at this time. Revising should be looked at as an opportunity to let student know if they are on track or if they need to rethink a problem. Allowing students to revise their work is a new concept for many mathematics teachers. If you have never done this before, you might want to have a conversation with one of the language arts teachers in your school and ask them how they orchestrate revision work for student writing since this is a common practice in that discipline.

The nature of the problems in these assessment pieces require that teachers readjust their expectation that 80% of the students will show 80% mastery. Rather, teachers will want to use holistic scoring techniques and multidimensional weighted grading scales that take into account the many dimensions addressed by the test. Teachers are encouraged to investigate many resources for aid in establishing scoring rubrics for these types of assessment. Some examples are: *Alternative*

Assessment in Mathematics from the EQUALS project, and *Mathematics Assessment—Myths, Models, Good Questions and Practical Suggestions* from the California Department of Education.

Example of **Quiz** question from the *Covering and Surrounding*—Grade 6.

Pizza shops often sell round pizzas in various prices. At Pizza Nook they sell the following sizes:

6 inch —— **$3.00**

12 inch —— **$8.00**

18 inch —— **$12.00**

2. The new manager of the Pizza Nook is thinking about changing the prices of pizzas. It appears to him that he could think about the pricing in three ways:

   I.   The prices of the pizzas are influenced by comparing the diameters.

   II. The prices of the pizzas are influenced by comparing the circumferences.

   III. The prices of the pizzas are influenced by comparing the areas.

   a) If you were the manager which method would be most appropriate for pricing the pizza?

   b) Explain your reasoning.

Projects

Several units incorporate projects in one of several forms: as a replacement for a unit test, in addition to a unit test, or as an integral part of a unit test—usually in take-home format. Projects are offered for those teachers who want to engage their students in tasks that are more product/performance based. Projects offered are open ended tasks that provide opportunities for students to engage in independent work and to demonstrate their broad understanding of ideas in the unit. Information about students' disposition toward engaging in mathematics can be gathered through this type of task. A set of Project guidelines are written for each project.

Example of **Project** guide from student materials of *Covering and Surrounding*—Grade 6.

Plan a Park Project

At the beginning of this unit, you read about Dr. Doolittle's donation of land to the city, which she designated as a new park. It is now time to design your plan for the piece of land. Use the information you have collected about parks, plus what you learned from your study of this unit, to prepare your final design.

Your design should satisfy the following constraints:
- The park should be rectangular with dimensions 120 yards by 100 yards.
- About half of the park should consist of a picnic area and a playground, but these two sections need not be located together.
- The picnic area should contain a circular flower garden. There should also be a garden in at least one other place in the park.
- There should be trees in several places in the park. Young trees will be planted, so your design should show room for the trees to grow.
- The park must appeal to families, so there should be more than just a picnic area and a playground.

Your design package should be neat, clear, and easy to follow. Your design should be drawn and labeled in black and white. In addition to a scale drawing of your design for the park, your project should include a report that gives:

1. the size (dimensions) of each item. These items should include gardens, trees, picnic tables, playground equipment, and anything else you included in your design.
2. the amount of land needed for each item and the calculations you used to determine the amount of land needed.
3. the materials needed. Include the amount of each item needed and the calculations you did to determine the amounts. Include the number and type of each piece of playground equipment, the amount of fencing, the numbers of picnic tables and trash containers, the amount of land covered by concrete or blacktop (so the developers can determine how much cement or blacktop will be needed), and the quantities of other items you included in your park.
4. a letter to Dr. Doolittle explaining why she should choose your design for the park. Include a justification for the choices you made about the size and quantity of items in your park.

An example of the **Teacher's Guide** for *Covering and Surrounding* Unit Project—6th Grade.

The Plan a Park Project is the final assessment for *Covering and Surrounding*. The project gives students an opportunity to think about the amount of area things occupy. They will need to use measurement skills, concepts of area and perimeter, and reasoning about size and space to create their design.

This project could be assigned as an individual, partner, or small-group project. Assign the project near the end of the unit (during or after Investigation 7). Although this project will take several hours to complete, most of the work could be done outside of class. You may want to take 15 to 20 minutes to launch the project in class and then have students finish the project as homework.

Read through the description of the unit project, which is on pages 82 and 83 of the student edition, with the class. Make sure everyone understands the project, including the idea that Dr. Doolittle is not asking that the park be divided into two parts, but that half the total area be reserved for what she has specified. The elements she requires—the playground area, the picnic area, the trees, and the circular flower garden—can be located anywhere in the park.

The Plan a Park Project is the final assessment in *Covering and Surrounding*. The project was introduced at the beginning of the unit. Students were told about a contest to design the layout of a city park. After each investigation, students were reminded to think about the concepts they were learning and how they might use these ideas in their park designs. They were also asked to visit local parks or school playgrounds and make measurements of things they might put in their designs.

The Plan a Park Project gives students an opportunity to think about the size of things and the amount of area they occupy. They will need to use measurement skills, concepts or area and perimeter, ideas of scaling, and reasoning about size and space to create their designs.

(continued)

The project could be assigned as an individual or partner project. An ample supply of grid paper, as well as calculators, rulers, measuring tapes, string, and compasses should be available for students to use as they conduct research for their park designs. (Gird paper on large rolls is available through teacher-supply catalogs or stores.) We recommend that students use grid paper with small squares because of the size of the park.

Read through the description of the unit project, which is on pages 82 and 83 of the student edition. Make sure everyone understands the project, including the idea that Dr. Doolittle is not asking that the park be divided into two parts, but that *half of the total area* be reserved for what she has specified. The elements she requires—the playground, the picnic area, the trees, and the circular flower garden—can be located anywhere in the park.

You will want to talk with your students about what it means to make a scale drawing. You could discuss how to set up a one-to-one scale with grid paper. For example, if students will be using centimeter grid paper, one centimeter on the grid paper could represent one yard of the park. Your students have been informally making scale drawings through out the unit, beginning with the tile models of bumper car floors. Because the audience for the design is more than the teacher, each design should include a key that gives the scaling ratio.

Although this project will take several hours to complete, most of the work can be done outside of class. You may want to take 10 or 15 minutes to launch the project in class and then a few minutes every couple of days to discuss questions your students have as they work on their projects. A week, including a weekend, is a reasonable amount of time to give students for this project.

Here are some common questions that students ask, along with suggested answers:

Q: How do I represent trees? Do I show the trunk or the spread of the branches?

A: Most landscape drawings are aerial views, so you should show the spread of the branches.

(continued)

Q: Do I have to show calculations for the numbers of trees and picnic tables?

A: No, you can just find these by counting. You need to include the counts for these items, but not an addition equation to show the sum of the tables and the trees.

Q: Do I have to give the perimeter *and* the area for each item in my park?

A: No, you should be selective about the measurements you include. For example, when you describe the amount of fencing needed for your park, you need only give perimeter. When you specify the amount of space needed for the picnic area, you need only give area.

Remind students that their reports should be organized so the reader can easily find information about items in the park. Giving students your grading rubric for the project should help them understand what they need to do.

Suggested Scoring Rubric

A total of 50 points is possible for the project—23 for the scale drawing, 22 for the report, and 5 for the letter to Dr. Doolittle.

Scale drawing

Dimensions and measurements—16 points
- dimensions are labeled (3 pts)
- dimensions are close to dimensions of actual items (9 pts.)
- scale is included (2 pts)
- design meets problem constraints (2 pts)

Complete design—7 points
- design is reasonable and logical (4 pts)
- design is neat, well-organized, and includes required items (3 pts)

Report

Mathematics—16 points
- dimensions are given and correctly match drawing (4 pts)
- calculations are correct (6 pts)

(continued)

- necessary and correct measurements are given with explanations of what the measurements mean and why they are need (6 pts)

Organization—6 points

- work is neat, easy to follow, and meets the requirements of the problem (3 pts)
- information is easy to find (3 pts)

Letter

Composition—3 points

- letter is easy to read and understand (1 pt)
- justifications are given for decisions (1 pt)
- reasons are given for why design should be chosen (1 pt)

Structure—2 points

- letter is neat (1 pt)
- grammar and spelling are correct (1 pt)

Unit Tests

Teachers should assume that tests are intended to be individual tests unless alternative directions are given in the unit. Test guidelines are given for those units where the test is of a non-traditional form. Some of the tests have been designed with a take-home format, some incorporate project level work and all tests feature some questions that are open.

Unit tests are provided to inform teachers about the ability of students to apply, refine, and modify their acquired mathematical knowledge to fit a variety of conditions. Unit tests have some questions that are summative of the unit and tend to be smaller and more skill oriented. They also have some problems that are more problem solving oriented and are asking students to do more than demonstrate the mathematical skills of the unit. The nature of the problems in these assessment pieces require that teachers readjust their expectation that 80% of the students will show 80% mastery. Rather, teachers will want to use holistic scoring techniques and multidimensional weighted grading scales that take into account the many dimensions addressed by the test.

Examples of **Unit Test** questions from *Bits and Pieces I*—Grade 6.

2. Write each of the following situations as a fraction, decimal, and percent.
   a) 30 days out of 100 days
   b) 55¢ compared to 100¢
   c) 20 correct out of 25 problems
   d) 3 out of 4 free-throws were made
   e) 21 mountain bikes out of 40 bikes
   f) 5 misspelled words out of 30 words

3. At the pizza shop, they sell 16 inch diameter pizzas for $9.85. They have decided to sell pizza by the slice and to sell small slices and large slices. The shop has a cutting form that can cut the pizza into 12 slice or another form that can cut a pizza into 8 slices.
   a) How much should they charge for the larger slice to make at least $9.85 on each whole pizza sold?
   b) How much should they charge for the small slice to make at least $9.85 on each whole pizza sold?
   c) Explain why you think your answers for a) and b) are appropriate.

Self-Assessment/"Show What You Know"

"Show What You Know" is the *CMP* label for the students self-assessment component. After every unit, students are asked to put together a written summary of the mathematics they have learned in the unit, ideas that they are still struggling with, and examples of how and what they did in class that added to the learning of the mathematics. The goal of this activity is to have students reflect on the mathematics they learned as a result of completing this unit. For many students, self-assessment is a new experience. Students struggle with this at first but with feedback from teachers and the sharing of fellow students' work as models, students can learn to reflect on their own sense making.

Example of **Self-Assessment** from *Covering and Surrounding*—Grade 6.

Show What You Know

Situations that involve **Covering** things (area) and **Surrounding** things are part of everyday life; floors are covered with carpeting and tile, yards are surrounded by fencing. After studying the mathematics in the unit **Covering and Surrounding,**

1. a) I learned these things about:
   - the relationship between area and perimeter
   - how to find area and perimeter of rectangles, parallelograms, triangles and circles

   b) Evidence of this can be found in my journal on pages _____. What each of these shows is:...

2. a) The mathematical idea(s) that I am still struggling with is (are)...

   b) These ideas are difficult for me because...

   c) Evidence of this can be found in my journal on pages _____. What this shows is...

Class Participation

I contributed to the classroom **discussion** and understanding of the **Covering and Surrounding** unit and the ideas about area and perimeter when {state example(s)}...

Question Bank

In addition to all the assessment items, the investigation problems, and the ACE problems; a bank of questions is given for each unit. These questions can be used for homework problems, class investigation problems, or substitute for some of the quiz and check-up questions. Some of the questions can be used to give students an additional opportunity to work on a set of ideas. Other questions are written as additional extension problems for teachers that want to go further with an idea from the unit.

E. A neighbor asks you to help her design a rectangular dog pen. Your neighbor has 42 meters of fencing.

1. What design gives the dog the most space for playing? Give the dimensions.

2. What design gives the dog the best space for running? Give the dimensions.

Your neighbor changes her mind and decides to use her house as one of the walls for the pen. Her house is 35 meters long.

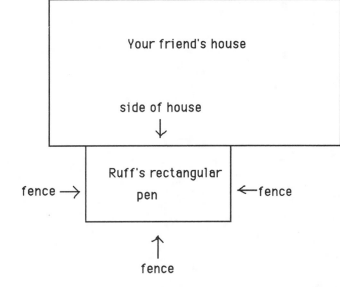

3. What design gives the most space for playing? Give the dimensions.

4. What design gives the best space for running? Give the dimensions.

ORGANIZATION TOOLS

Notebooks

One successful organizational tool for many *CMP* teachers has been student mathematics notebooks. They have found this helps their students with the organization of their materials and are thus more prepared for some of the demanding tasks embedded in the curriculum materials. Using a three-ring binder for these notebook seems to be working well. It allows students to easily take thing in and out and organize the material to their advantage. We suggest notebooks as an organizational tool but are not saying they are a mandate.

Notebooks can be used as a place for students to keep all their work and materials. Teachers recommend that notebooks be comprised of the following sections: journal (see description below), vocabulary, homework, assessment items, and *CMP* textbook. By dividing the notebook into sections, students can easily access the information they need.

Notebook Check

A notebook check is offered with each unit. It is a tool for students to use to check the completeness of their notebook before turning them into the teacher to survey and grade or not. Some teachers give the notebook check to students at the beginning of a unit to remind them what they are to have in their notebook.

Example of a Notebook-Check sheet for *Covering and Surrounding*—Grade 6.

Covering and Surrounding
Notebook Check

✓ (have)

A. Journal Organization
_____ 1. Investigation problems and reflections identified and dated
_____ 2. Work neat, easy to find and follow

B. Vocabulary
_____ 1. all words listed
_____ 2. all words defined or described
3. The word(s) that best demonstrate my ability to give a clear and complete definition or description is (are) _____
4. The word(s) that best demonstrate my ability to use an example to make the definition or description is (are) _____

C. Assessment Organization
_____ 1. Check-Up #1
_____ 2. Quiz A
_____ 3. Check-Up #2
_____ 4. Quiz B
5. Homework:

Assignments

_____

_____

_____

_____

_____

_____

_____

_____

_____

_____

_____

Vocabulary Lists

Vocabulary lists are given for each unit. The lists contains the mathematical vocabulary used through the unit. Words with an "E" in front of them denote those words that are viewed as essential that students understand for use in this unit and for future *CMP* units. Some teachers chose to hand out the provided list to their class. Other teachers have their class generate a vocabulary list for each unit and they use the given *CMP* list as a guide. To highlight this section and to help students organize this information, some teachers have given their students colored sheets of paper, that match the color of the book that the students are working in, to record their vocabulary words and definitions.

The philosophy of *CMP* is that during the course of study for the unit, students develop definitions for each of the words. Because students' definitions may change and grow, students should be encouraged to leave space between their list of words for revisions.

Below is a copy of what one teacher handed out to her students as a guide to keeping their vocabulary section.

Student Guidelines for Vocabulary Section of Notebook

Vocabulary development is:

- For personal and class development of mathematical vocabulary as the need arises.

In your vocabulary section you should have the following:

- Any and all words that we as a class agree needs to be in everyone's notebook vocabulary section.
- For each word recorded, a definition/description needs to be given by the end of study of the unit.
- Definitions/descriptions can use words, charts, pictures, examples, and anything else to help make clear what the word means in our mathematics community

To help you organize your journal for yourself and for me (the teacher) when I go through it, please do the following:

- Underline each vocabulary word listed
- Leave room between words for a definition/description and space for revisions.
- Always revise what you have written by "✗-ing out" rather than erasing. This saves time and helps me to follow your thinking. It does not count against you to "✗-out" work.

Example of **Vocabulary List** from *Covering and Surrounding*—Grade 6.

Covering And Surrounding Vocabulary

E 1. Area
E 2. Perimeter
E 3. Circle
E 4. Diameter
E 5. Radius (radii)
E 6. Circumference
   7. Pentomino
   8. Perpendicular
E 9. (Circle) center

Note: "E" denotes those vocabulary words that are viewed as essential that students understand for use in this unit and for future *CMP* units.

Know how these terms are used.

10. (Linear dimensions)
   a) length
   b) width
   c) base
   d) height

Vocabulary developed in previous units.

11. Square
12. Rectangle
13. Parallelogram
14. Triangle
15. Octagon
16. Hexagon
17. Trapezoid
18. Regular polygon
19. Dimensions
20. Line plot

Journals

Another successful tool that teachers used was journals. The journal was a place for students to keep notes, solve the investigation problems, and record their mathematical reflections.

The role of journal entries for student assessment should be one of completeness rather than correctness. Journals are to be a safe place for students to try out their thinking. Language Arts teachers have used journals to a greater degree generally than mathematics teachers, and their experience generally supports the assessment of journals for completeness.

Below is a copy of what one teacher handed out to her students as a guide to using their journal.

Student Guidelines for Mathematics Journal

Journals are—for personal use on a daily basis. In your journal you should have the following:

- Any and *all work you do for in-class problems* (those are usually the investigation problems from your textbook). Include words, charts, pictures, or anything else to show your thinking.
- *Any notes that you take.* You should write anything and everything that will help you remember what you are thinking and that you can refer back to and can help you with homework and class problems.
- Your *Mathematical Reflections* from each investigation.

To help you organize your journal for yourself and for me (the teacher) when I go through it, please do the following:

- Date every entry and identify problems you are working on with problem numbers and unit name.
- Always revise what you have written by "✗-ing out" rather than erasing. This saves time and helps me to follow your thinking. It does not count against you to "✗ out" work.

Using Assessment for Reporting

Below is one teacher's grading scheme for her *CMP* mathematics classes. This is given as an example of a possible grading scheme.

Grading Scheme for *CMP* Classes

Journals (part of the "Notebook")
Collect student journals from notebooks, once a week

Scoring Rubric for Journals

5 work for all investigation problems (done in class, to date) and reflections present, labeled, easy to find and follow

4 most class work and reflections present, labeled, and easy to find and follow

3 some missing class work or reflections, teacher needs to work to find and follow student work.

Below a 3 is not acceptable. Students have to come in at lunch or after school and meet with the teacher and work on their journal until it is at least at a 3 level.

Participation
Participation means questioning, listening, and offering ideas.

Students are given a participation grading sheet every Monday. These are to be handed in on Friday. Students are to fill these out through out the week, giving evidence of their participation in the class. On the sheets they are to note:

- when and how they contribute to the class discussion
- when they use an idea from the class discussion and revise their work or their thinking.

Scoring Rubric for Participation

5 student has made an extra effort to participate and help others in the class to understand the mathematics. Student gave evidence of participating all 5 days of the week.

4 student made an effort to participate, giving evidence of at least 4 days of participation for the week.

3 student made some effort to participate, giving evidence of at least 3 days of class participation for the week.

Below a 3 is not acceptable. Teacher talks with student about their lack of effort. If no improvement is seen in the next week, a parent or guardian is called and informed of the problem.

Homework (selected ACE questions)

(In this teacher's class) before homework is checked or collected, students are given the opportunity to ask questions about the assignment. The teacher does not give answers or tell how to solve the problem but, with the classes help, tries to work with students to understand what the question is asking. Students have the right to revise any of their work while this conversation is going on and not be marked down. Grading is strict on this work because students have had the opportunity to take care of themselves and get help.

Scoring Rubric for Homework

✓+ close to perfect

✓ all problems attempted, most work done correctly

✓- most problems attempted, some given answers are wrong or not complete

✓- not much work, most work that is given is wrong or not complete

0 no work

Check-Ups, Partner Quizzes, and Unit Tests

(With partner quizzes, only the revised paper, that turned in the second time, is scored for a grade.)

Scoring Rubric for Check-Ups, Partner Quizzes, and Unit Tests

Each assessment has its own point marking scheme devised by the teacher. Points are determined by the amount of work asked for to solve each problem. Not all problems are awarded the same number of points.

Projects

A six-point holistic rubric is used for all projects.

Scoring Rubric for Projects

5 Project is complete, mathematics is correct, work is neat and easy
to follow.

4 Project is mostly complete, most of the mathematics is correct, work is
neat and easy enough to follow.

3 Project has some missing pieces, some of the mathematics is correct, it
takes some effort by the teacher to follow the work.

2 Project is missing some major parts, there are several problems with the
mathematics, it takes extra effort on the teacher's part to follow
the work.

1 Little to no significant work.

0 No project turned in.

Assigning grades to numbers 0–5 and marks 0 to ✓+.

5s and ✓+	As
4s and ✓	Bs
3s and ✓-	Cs
2s and ✓- -	Ds
1s and **0**s	Es

IDEAS FOR PORTFOLIO ASSESSMENT AND *CMP*

Portfolio assessment most often involves the use of curriculum-based tasks that
provide opportunities for students to show what they know and can do in
mathematical processes, content topics, and reflection/self-assessment. *CMP*
provides excellent tasks for teachers and students to select from to build their
assessment portfolios. Below, different aspects of the *CMP* curriculum and
assessment are cited to help you begin identifying tasks that have good potential as
portfolio entries.

Documenting Mathematical Processes

(Problem Solving, Reasoning, Communication and Connections)

Finding tasks that can provide students with opportunities to solve problems, reason and/or communicate is not difficult in *CMP*. For example, in the assessment package, the **Quizzes** are designed to just this! Written for students to do in pairs, these **Quizzes** reflect a commitment to assessment that promotes further learning while taking a quiz. Take a look at the Pizza Nook problem example on Page 46 of this guide. This problem provides an opportunity for students to reason about measurement and rates. They are asked to take on the role of manager in solving the problem and to explain their reasoning.

End of Unit Projects can also be used in portfolios to provide evidence of students' problem solving, reasoning and communication. The sample **project** on page 58 of this guide illustrates how *CMP* involves students in long term projects. In this example, students need to use scale drawing in their development of a plan for a park. **Projects** in the *CMP* curriculum are intended to be done individually over a 4 to 6 week period. These types of products can be used in portfolios to represent extended work by the students. Another source of extended tasks can be found in the **Extension** section of the **ACE** problems at the end of each unit. These examples provide opportunities for students to investigate more deeply the mathematics addressed in the unit. Often, students are required to develop definitions, formulate questions, conduct an exploration and/or make a case for their findings, as in the **Extension** problem on page 37 of this guide, which provides starting points from which students can launch their own investigations.

Problems from the investigations in the student texts can also lend themselves for use in portfolio assessment. For example the Sole D'Italia Pizzeria problem requires students to CONNECT a real world idea of "fairness" to an analysis of a numerical and measurement situation. Students would need to define "fair," apply their criterion of "fair," and make a case for the position they are taking. (See Page 34 of this guide.)

The **Connections** section in the **ACE** of the student text is designed to have students CONNECT recently learned mathematics to mathematics addressed in previous units. For example, the following illustration is from the 6th Grade *Covering and Surrounding* unit. It deals with dimensions and area, but the context refers back to geometric representations of a product and its factors in the unit, reflecting connections to the *Prime Time* unit.

7. Kate and Doug are designing garages that have an area of 240 square feet.

   a) Make an organized list showing the length and width (the dimensions) of all the possible rectangular garages they could design with whole number dimensions.

   b) Identify which ones would be reasonable for a garage and explain why.

   c) Which rectangle would you choose for a garage and why?

Tasks like these can be used in conjunction with reflection prompts asking students to explicitly identify the connections they see being made among the problems they have solved, investigations they have completed, mathematics they know and real world situations they have encountered. Their solutions to the tasks, along with a discussion of connections, will provide rich entries to assessment portfolios.

Content Topics

Each unit of the *CMP* program deals with a few "big ideas" that are central to the focus. By selecting a balance of tasks from across the units, students can build portfolios that represent the various mathematics strands outlined in the *NCTM Standards*. In particular, the **Applications** section of the **ACE** may be used by students to illustrate their understanding and skill in specific topics of mathematics. An example **Application** problem on page 35 of this guide deals with area and circumference of circles in contexts not used in the Investigation. This task also provides an opportunity for students to make CONNECTIONS between mathematics and the real world as well. The **Applications** sections can be searched for items that address content strands and mathematical processes simultaneously.

The **Question Bank** is another source of tasks that students can use to demonstrate their understanding of the big ideas in the unit. The questions are of various forms: skill-level to investigations, and can thus be used to represent many aspects as a portfolio.

Reflection and Self-Assessment

Students need to understand the "new rules" of the assessment game. They are now being asked to produce portfolios that provide evidence of their performance in problem solving, reasoning, communication and connections. Rather than including a large number of tasks with single right answers, portfolio producers are being asked to identify work that illustrates how they found multiple methods to solve a problem, or multiple solutions based on different assumptions about the situation. One way to help students learn the new criterion for mathematical performance is to introduce self-assessment through a variety of reflective experiences. The **"Show What You Know"** piece in the student text asks students to reflect on their contribution to the mathematical community in their classroom and their own personal growth in knowledge. Illustrated on Page 64 of this guide is how the prompts for **"Show What You Know"** are specific to the "big ideas" in the particular unit, and provides opportunities for students to reflect on how well they are meeting the expectations of the curriculum. Students' write-ups can provide reflective, SELF-ASSESSMENT pieces for use in their assessment portfolios.

Another way SELF-ASSESSMENT can be addressed is by focusing on the **Mathematical Highlights** at the beginning of each unit. Students who keep a journal can begin a unit by reflecting on what they already know about the questions posed. (For example, see Page 33 of this guide.) They can revisit the questions at the end of the unit and be asked to reflect on their growth over the unit, pointing out what they can do now that they didn't know or couldn't do before.

Within units, students can assess what they are learning by using the **Reflection** questions that are provided at the end of the investigation to help students summarize the big ideas. For example, on Page 39 in this guide, students are asked to articulate how they can find perimeter and area of circles in general. By providing a problem without numbers, the students need to pull together their understanding of the concepts and procedures to respond to the general questions.

Getting Started

If you have already begun to implement assessment portfolios in your classroom, the ideas from the above discussion will serve you well. If you haven't yet started, don't feel overwhelmed! Begin by introducing a focus on one area with which you feel comfortable, such as COMMUNICATION or PROBLEM SOLVING. Start the year by developing a definition of the COMMUNICATION collaboratively with students. Together look for examples of student work that provides evidence of COMMUNICATION. Help students select tasks to include in a "working portfolio." Together with the students, develop criterion that will be used to evaluate the COMMUNICATION aspect in of their portfolio tasks. Assess student products jointly using the criteria so that both you and your students develop similar understandings about how performance will be evaluated. Finally, select the pieces from the working portfolio to include in the final portfolio.

Later in the year select another aspect to investigate, such as PROBLEM SOLVING or CONNECTIONS. As above, you and the students together will need to define what is meant by the process, together search for examples of student work that illustrate performance with that process, collaboratively develop criteria to evaluate student performance with the mathematical process, use the criteria collaboratively to assess student work, and finally select pieces to include in the final portfolio that illustrate the students' performance and/or growth in that process area.

It may take one, two or three years before you feel as if you have a sound grasp of how to help students begin developing portfolios. This is normal, because it is not simply asking students to put some papers in a folder. Rather, documenting higher ordered thinking processes is asking both you and your students to develop a whole new way of thinking about the nature of mathematics and what "evidence" of mathematical performance is. Take your time, be prepared to feel like a beginning teacher again, and allow the process of change to take its own natural course. Students will also need some time to understand what the new expectations are. You will find the rewards of portfolio assessment to be motivating to your students as well as to you in your professional development. An additional reward has been reported by *CMP* field test teachers who have used portfolios in parent conferences. Parents are reportedly interested in their youngster's actual work and discussions about what the work reveals about the student's learning and to what extent the student's performance meets the criterion. While parents still want to know about their child's grades, the discussion repeatedly returns to the student's actual performance on tasks rather than just discussion how grades are computed.

One last suggestion, implement portfolios along with a colleague. The opportunity to talk about the process, exchange ideas, and reflect on classroom experiences will be rewarding and revealing!

A Teacher's Use of Partner Quizzes

Using Partner Quizzes

by Sarah Theule-Lubienski

As I taught 7th Grade this past year, I tried various forms and uses of partner quizzes. Although my philosophy will not fit everyone's situation, I thought it might be useful to share some of the ways I found useful for using partner quizzes.

When I Used Partner Quizzes

I did not use partners for every occasion. I found that I was most comfortable using partners for the quiz in the middle of the unit and not for the final test of the unit. Through student interviews I conducted this year, I learned that some students find quizzes and tests useful for helping them see what the really important ideas in a unit are. Hence, the quiz that I usually give in the middle of the unit is a good place for students to work with a partner—this allows students to realize both what the key ideas are and what assessment on these ideas can look like in a less stressful situation. It also allows students the opportunity to learn important ideas from their partner.

However, I do think that it is important for students, parents, and teachers to see what students are capable of doing on their own. After students have experienced a partner quiz over some of the key ideas in the unit, they have some idea of the types of questions that might be asked on a test. Hence, I think partner quizzes help better prepare my students for taking the unit test individually.

Partner Formation

I allowed students to choose their own partners, and I also gave students the option of working alone. Initially I was concerned about doing this, since I feared that students would fight, feelings would be hurt, time would be wasted, the "smart" kids would always pair up with other "smart" kids or choose to work alone, etc. But I found that many of my fears were needless and I also found ways to deal with some of my fears that were not.

Generally speaking, students were excited about working together, and they were able to choose partners quickly. The "smart" kids did not choose to work alone, and often the kids who were usually considered to be "geeks" were suddenly rather popular with the "cool" kids, which made them feel good, I think. Sometimes there were "leftover" kids who did not have partners. In this case, I allowed them to make a threesome with any pair they chose, or work on their own. If they chose to work on their own (and occasionally I felt that some students did make this choice because they were unsure how welcome they would [be] by other students), I would often give them a bit of extra care during the quiz-taking time. Hence, for these individuals, I played the role of a pseudo-partner of sorts—probing and questioning at key points where it was likely to be helpful to the student.

Grading

I was happy when I realized that grades on partner quizzes are, on average, about 10–15% higher than they are on individual quizzes or tests. Each student wrote up [his/] her own answers, and I did not force students to agree on their answers. I gave each student an individual grade. Still, to try to cut down on the amount of grading I had to do, I asked students to indicate on the front of their tests which questions they disagreed about. This seemed to work out well, except that I found that sometimes students thought they agreed on every question, but if I happened to look at both papers, there were some important disagreements (that seemed minor to the student). When I noticed these discrepancies, I chose to grade each paper separately. Still, I continued to encourage students to carefully compare their answers. The development of students' abilities to make critical comparisons of their answers could be considered an important side-benefit of partner quizzes.

Communicating with Students and Parents

Students were constantly asking to take everything as partners. I found that I needed to become clear in my own mind about why I made certain decisions about when and how to use the partner quiz idea. As I became more clear about these issues, I was up-front with my students about my philosophy and how that affected the decisions I was making. I believe that sharing instructional philosophies with students can help them make better sense and use of their learning environments.

I was surprised, but I had no parental comments or complaints about partner quizzes. To be honest, I was not quick to bring it up with them, for fear of the reaction I would get. But I now feel that I have a sensible, defensible philosophy to share with parents, and in the future I would try to be up-front with parents, as well as students, about this philosophy.

V. Implementing *CMP*:
What It Takes to Make *CMP* Work

Teacher

The *Connected Mathematics Project* assumes that teachers will need support in implementing a problem–centered curriculum that changes the work and expectations of both students and teachers in the classroom. Since the curriculum includes areas of mathematics that may be new to the teacher and investigates familiar material in greater depth, teachers may need help in acquiring the mathematical knowledge needed to teach these materials. Another area that teachers will need time and opportunity to work on is new kinds of assessments, such as partner quiz, and project evaluation. The *CMP* student and teacher materials provide a great deal of help for a teacher. However, changing practice and implementing a new curriculum is hard work. Having time to plan with other teachers, to share ideas, to share frustrations, and perhaps, to watch each other teach, is critical to the success of such an implementation. As you plan to use *CMP* materials for the first time, try to establish a support system for all the teachers in a building that will be working to use the material. At the least find a buddy on the staff that will work with you to support each other in the implementation of a new curriculum with new expectations.

Student

The *Connected Mathematics Project* assumes that when all students are held to the same high expectations and given a chance to explore rich problems, all students can succeed in mathematics. We assume that students coming into *CMP* at Grade 6 have a firm grasp of whole numbers, some understanding of the part-whole interpretation of fraction and the place value interpretation of decimals, and some acquaintance with geometry and measurement. Whole numbers will be revisited in many different investigations in the *CMP*. In addition, rational number concepts, geometry, algebra, measurement, probability and statistics will be explored in depth.

The Classroom

In addition to high expectations for all students, students need the time to explore the rich problem solving situations and to develop their understandings in a variety of ways. The *CMP* curriculum assumes that there will be sufficient time for the class to explore problems. Very often in classes with less than 45 minutes there is not time to make significant progress on a problem. Consequently, during the next class period the teacher and the students must repeat much of the exploration and discussion of the previous day before they can continue their work.

A comparison of the amount of time available for instruction in a 40 minute period and a 50 minute period shows that the latter class will have 25 to 30 hours more of instruction per year—or 6–8 weeks more of instruction time. If additional time per week cannot be allocated to mathematics, then the time should be broken into four longer periods a week rather than five shorter sessions. In addition to the length of the class period, schools must monitor the number of days that are actually spent teaching mathematics. We acknowledge that there will be days for field trips, assemblies, tests, professional days, etc. But in many schools the number of days spent teaching mathematics is less than 150 days out of the 180 day school year.

The *CMP* material is rich enough so that the need for extra materials such as classroom openers, problems of the week, or extra drill is diminished. However, the materials themselves can be used to provide classroom openers, problems of the week, or extra drill if you judge that your students need these kinds of activities. Time for mathematics is so precious in the middle school classroom that it must be effectively used to focus on mathematics.

Parents

Parent involvement in a student's education is an important factor in the student's success. In a program that is new and unfamiliar, such as Connected Math Project, parent involvement and support is even more important than in traditional programs. Being proactive about keeping parents informed, and about answering parent concerns will be a long term benefit, and is worth the extra time spent at the beginning stages.

Letters

Both students and parents need to be clear about the goals of the program so that there will not be any unnecessary frustration, stemming from miscommunication. These goals can be communicated to parents in several ways. A letter from the teacher to the parent(s) at the beginning of the school year should alert parents to the exciting and challenging new program in which the student is enrolled. This information could also be shared at a parent meeting. This is an appropriate time to inform parents of overall goals, and to point out ways in which *CMP* differs significantly from some traditional programs. Parents need to know that the goal is to have students make sense of the mathematics they study and to be able to communicate their reasoning clearly. The concepts and topics that students study should sound familiar to parents, and reassure them that significant and challenging mathematics is being studied. The emphasis on reasoning, however, may be unfamiliar to parents, and both parents and students need to understand that reasoning and communication are valued, and students will have many opportunities to demonstrate their progress in these areas.

As the school year progresses the need to communicate to parents shifts to include more specific information. Follow-up letters throughout the year can indicate what topics are being studied. Parents will have questions about how they can help their students, and general advice about how to help students communicate reasoning more effectively, as well as specific advice about activities parents can enjoy with their children will be welcome.

Example from a parent letter for *Shapes and Designs*—Grade 6 unit.

Ways that you can work with your student to help him/her get the most out of this unit:

- Point out different shapes you see and ask your student to find different shapes when you are together.
- Every couple of days, or when you notice an interesting shape in the newspaper or a magazine, point out one of the specific polygons that your child is to investigate and ask if they might want to cut it out and save it to use for their shapes project.
- Have your student share with you their mathematics notebook, showing you what they have recorded about the different shapes they have studied and explain why these ideas are important.
- Look over your student's homework and make sure all questions are answered and that explanations are clear.

A complete sample letter for the beginning of the year and one for during the year are included in Appendix A.

Parent Meetings

Several schools have found parent meetings a good avenue for helping parents learn about their children's mathematics program. Sixth Grade teachers or schools that are in their first year of implementation of this new program, have found these meetings to be helpful.

In the districts that have offered parent meetings, teachers conduct their first meeting in the early fall, one or two weeks into the school year. The meetings are planned for an hour and a half in the evening and are run by the teacher. At the meeting the parents are given a short overview of the program but then asked to take the role of their student and to engage in some of the problems from the first unit. With 6th Grade parents this often involves having the parents play the two games from *Prime Time*. The teacher draws the parents back together after they have played the games and points out the mathematics involved in playing the game. An overview of the remainder of the unit and the goals for the unit are addressed in this summary. A question and answer period follows. This format is used two, three, and four times a year in some districts, each time working with the parents on the unit their child is currently studying.

One common parental concern is the use of graphics calculators. While both meetings and letters are valid forms of communicating to parents, at a meeting parents can have the opportunity to try out this impressive technology. When parents see the level of mathematics that is made accessible through the uses of these machines, their discomfort is allayed at the way this unfamiliar technology is integrated into the program. This would also be an ideal time to discuss ways to make calculators available to all students.

When Parents Say They Can't Help Their Students

By the time students get to middle school, teachers begin to hear from parents that they cannot help their students with their mathematics. This concern is often heightened when a new program is introduced, especially one that is so different from the way the parents learned mathematics. What some districts have done to address this concern is offer "After School Mathematics Tutoring Lab." The way this plays out in one district is: Mathematics Lab is held two days a week after school. Students sign up to attend with their mathematics teacher. When students come to lab they need to have something to do. This might involve working on homework that is due the next day, working on a past assignment that they had trouble with and want more help on, organizing their notebook and working on sections such as their vocabulary, studying for a test or quiz, or working on a project. In this school there is one teacher in charge of the lab. The tutors are high school students who come to the middle school for this purpose. Tutors are chosen because of their strong mathematics and their ability to work with other people. Several of the tutors are members of the National Honor Society and their work at the lab counts towards their service work. In the lab are copies of all the units and teacher editions as well as other materials you would find in any mathematics classroom. The mathematics lab is seen as one more piece of what it takes to make a strong program and offer all students an opportunity to learn.

How Well Is *CMP* Working for Students?

The primary question that anyone—parents, teachers, administrators—must ask about any mathematics curriculum is what do students learn from studying such a curriculum. The preliminary evidence gathered during the piloting of *CMP* indicates that students in *CMP* classes are performing well in conceptual development, problem solving, and other higher order thinking measures. Because the curriculum does not emphasize arithmetic computations done by hand, some *CMP* students may not do as well on parts of standardized tests assessing computational skills as students in classes that spend most of their time on practicing such skills. We believe such a trade-off in favor of *CMP* is very much to students' advantage in both the world of work and in continued study of mathematics. This does not mean that *CMP* does not value students' developing skill with operations. On the contrary, *CMP* focuses on making sense of operations and when they are useful to solve a problem. However, calculators are available to perform computation with larger numbers. Mental strategies for estimating numerical computations are developed through benchmarks for fractions, decimals, and percents. These benchmarks and their relationships are practiced for instant recall and recognition. For example, students learn to place a fraction such as $\frac{7}{8}$ between the benchmarks $\frac{3}{4}$ and 1. This means that $2\frac{1}{5} + \frac{7}{8}$ will be close to 3. Students also learn such benchmarks as $\frac{1}{8}$ as a decimal is 0.125 and as a percent is 12.5%. This allows students to flexible move between decimals, fractions and percents and to make judgments about numbers that are close to $\frac{1}{8}$. This theme of benchmarks continues in other units, for example, *Data Around Us*, which develops students' estimation skill with and understanding of large numbers.

At present, we are engaged in a large scale comparative study of *CMP* students versus control classes from 15 sites around the country. These sites are located in 9 different states with multiple sites in several of the states. There are 1,000 *CMP* students at Grades 6 and 7 and 500 control students at each grade level chosen from the 15 sites. We are collecting pre-post measures on all students on the Iowa Test of Basis Skills, a Middle School Test developed by the external evaluation team of *CMP* to reflect the most important mathematical ideas of the Middle Grades curriculum, and three performance tasks developed by the Balanced Assessment Team for the Middle Grades. Balanced Assessment is a National Science Foundation funded project that is developing balanced assessment packages to reflect the *NCTM Standards* in mathematics. We will complete comparative testing in 1996.

In addition to the current evaluation study of students' mathematical performance in *CMP* classes compared to non-*CMP* classes, the evaluation team has gathered data from teachers and students in *CMP* pilot classes over the past four years. This data has been used to revise the curriculum materials and the materials for teachers. Each grade level goes through three years of trials with revisions after each year. From these trials, the indications are that students in *CMP* are making substantial progress in learning to reason about situations that involve mathematics. Students are learning to solve problems, to look for patterns, to make conjectures, to create arguments to support their reasoning. Students are able to construct clear explanations of how they tackled a problem, as well as an explanation of what they found, and why they think they are correct. There is more writing in the *CMP* mathematics classes and teachers are setting higher expectations for students. Teachers tell us that *CMP* students keep surprising them about what they can learn and can do with the mathematics that they are learning. From what we have found so far, we feel confident that teachers and schools that implement *CMP*, will see growth of students over time in their problem solving skill, reasoning, connecting, and communication skills that make the hard work of implementing a new curriculum well worth the effort.

VI. Appendices:

APPENDIX A:

SAMPLE LETTERS TO PARENTS

Beginning of the Year Letter

Dear Parent or Guardian,

Welcome to the start of a new school year! We are excited about being back in the classroom and are looking forward to a good year. This letter is to introduce you to the 6th Grade mathematics program here at _____.

Overview of the Curriculum

This year students will be studying mathematics from the *Connected Mathematics Project* materials. The materials are structured into units that take 4 to 6 weeks each. Each unit is focused around problem situations that help students to learn an important set of related mathematical ideas and to become skillful at using these ideas to solve problems. The curriculum is structured to help students learn to communicate their strategies and their reasoning so that their mathematical understandings are much deeper. The kinds of problems that the student will work on in class, as well as for homework, are more challenging and interesting that they may have experienced in the past. Practice with ideas is provided throughout the units in the Application – Connections – Extensions problems assigned for classwork and homework. Our main goal is to help more and more of our students to be successful in and want to continue to study mathematics as they proceed through the grades.

The First Unit

The first unit of study is called **Prime Time.** In this unit students will learn about factors, multiples, divisors, products, primes, composites, common multiples, common factors and many other ideas about number. Because this is the first unit in Grade 6, it is also designed to help students learn what is expected in a curriculum that has been developed to build understanding of mathematics through investigation of problem situations. Students will have opportunities to work individually, in pairs, in small cooperative groups, and in whole class mode. They will be asked questions that call for explanations and justifications for their solutions. They will be engaged in writing about their ideas on a more frequent basis. In addition, in some of the units, they will be engaged in project work that will bring together all that they have learned in a unit. In this unit the project is called "My Special Number." The project is started at the beginning of the unit when each student picks his/her special number. Throughout the unit the students continue to apply each new idea they learn to their special number. By the end of the unit each student will have recorded a great deal of information about the properties of the special number. They will then design a project presentation of what they have found out about their special number.

Strategies for Helping Your Student

You can do a great deal to help your student succeed in mathematics. Here are some strategies that can be used throughout the year with any of the mathematics units.

- Encourage your student to do his or her homework on a regular basis.
- Have your student show you his or her mathematics notebook and explain to you what they have been doing in class.
- Have your student explain to you what each word in the vocabulary section of the notebook means to him/her. If your student is struggling with any words, together you might look the words up in a dictionary or look through the unit to get a better idea of what each means.
- Encourage your student by showing him or her that you believe that they can succeed if they try and work hard at the assignments.

We are looking forward to a successful year for all of our students. We are excited about this first unit and all the other units in the curriculum. If you have any questions or concerns at any time during the year, please feel free to call.

Sample of a During the Year Unit Letter

Dear Parent or Guardian,

This letter is to update you on your student's course of study this year in mathematics class. Our next unit is called ***Shapes and Designs***. It is a unit on geometry that teaches students about properties of shapes and relationships between shapes. The unit engages students in a series of activities that allow them to discover many of the key properties of polygonal shapes that make such shapes useful. This is the first unit in the *Connected Mathematics Project* on geometry. The unit goals include developing students' ability to recognize, analyze, and measure lengths of sides and angles of shapes.

As part of the assessment for this unit, students are asked to do a project on the common polygons they work with in the unit; triangles, squares, rectangles, parallelograms, quadrilaterals, pentagons, hexagons, and octagons. Throughout the unit they are asked to record what they learn about each polygon (its properties) and how the polygons relate to each other. Students are also asked to find examples of places where these different shapes can be found in their world.

Strategies for helping your student work with this unit:

- Point out different shapes you see and ask your student to find different shapes when you are together.
- When you notice an interesting shape in the newspaper or a magazine, point out one of the specific polygons that your child is to investigate and ask if he/she might want to cut it out and save it to use for the shapes project.
- Have your student share with you his/her mathematics notebook, showing you what has been recorded about the different shapes studied and explaining why these ideas are important.
- Look over your student's homework and make sure all questions are answered and that explanations are clear.

As always, if you have any questions or concerns about geometry or your student's progress in the class, please feel free to call. We all are interested in your child and want to maximize his/her mathematical experiences.

APPENDIX B:

OVERHEADS AND EXAMPLES OF ACTIVITIES FOR PARENT OR OTHER PUBLIC PRESENTATIONS ON THE *CMP* CURRICULUM

Outline of a One Hour Presentation on *CMP*

I.   (10 minutes) An overview of the *Connected Mathematics Project*
     Choose from the transparency masters provided:
     - The Overall Goals of *CMP*
     - The Mathematical Strands of *CMP*
     - The Curriculum Units of *CMP* for all Grade Levels
     - Features of the Students' Materials
     - Features of the Teachers' Materials

II. (30 minutes) Use the problem for your grade level and engage the parents in a "sample" class.
     Grade 6: Problem 7.2 from *Covering and Surrounding*.
     Grade 7: Problem 5.2 from *Comparing and Scaling*
     Grade 8: Problem 1.1 from *Thinking with Mathematical Models*

     Launch the problem using your own ideas or those suggested in the teachers' edition. Be sure to include a short summary of the goals of the unit from which the problem is taken.

     Put the audience into groups of 2 to 4 people to *explore* the problem. Have on hand all materials needed to explore the problem and summarize group work.

     Summarize the problem by having some groups report what they found, how they thought about the problem, what strategy they used to help solve the problem, and why they think they are correct. Be sure to stand back with the parents and look at the big mathematical ideas embedded in the problem. If you have student work on the problem, this is a good time to show some examples.

III. (10 minutes) Show examples of assessment, both informal and formal, that are provided to show what is expected of students and how you will monitor learning. Talk about your expectations for classwork and for homework. Talk about how parents can help. (See the parent letters for some ideas.)

IV. (10 minutes) Answer Questions.

Connected Mathematics Project Overall Goals

- Identifying big mathematical ideas around which to focus instruction

- Building on big ideas– making connections

- Teaching to support students development of deep understanding of and skill in using concepts and strategies

- Assessing student understandings in multiple ways

What Mathematical Strands Are Studied?

Number

Geometry

Measurement

Statistics

Probability

Algebra
Patterns – Relationships – Functions

Features
of Student Materials

- "Think About This" Questions

- Mathematical Goals for the Students

- Investigations

    ✔ Problems

    ✔ Homework: Applications – Connections – Extensions

    ✔ Mathematical Reflections

Features
of Teacher Materials

Overview of
- Big Mathematical Ideas of Unit and Investigations

- Mathematical and Problem Solving Goals

- Material and Time-lines for the Unit

Teaching Notes for Each Investigation
- Instructional Strategies for the:
    Launch – Explore – Summarize Phases

- Appropriate ACE Assignment

- Sample of Student Responses to Questions

- Complete Solutions to Investigations and
  ACE Questions and Reflections

Assessment
- Check–ups
- Projects
- Quiz Bank
- Quizzes
- Self-Assessment

Appendices
- Blackline Masters

- Students' Work and Scoring Suggestions

- Descriptive Glossary/Index

Curriculum

6th Grade	7th Grade	8th Grade
Prime Time Number Theory; primes; composites, factors and multiples	***Variables and Patterns*** Introducing Algebra; variables, tables, graphs, and symbols as representations	***Thinking with Mathematical Models*** Introduction to Functions and Modeling
Data About Us Data Investigation; Formulating questions, gathering data, organizing and analyzing data, making decisions based on data	***Stretching and Shrinking*** Similarity with congruence as a special case	***Looking for Pythagoras*** Pythagorean Theorem, slope, area and irrational numbers
Shapes and Designs Reasoning about shapes and shape properties; angle measure	***Comparing and Scaling*** Rate, Ratio, Proportion, Percent and Proportional Reasoning	***Growing, Growing, Growing...*** Exponential Growth
Bits and Pieces, Part I Understanding Rational Numbers: Fractions, Decimals, and Percents	***Accentuate the Negative*** Understanding and Using Integers	***Frogs, Fleas, and Painted Cubes*** Quadratic Growth
Covering and Surrounding Measurement: Area and Perimeter	***Moving Straight Ahead*** Linear Relationships expressed in words, tables, graphs, and symbols	***Say It With Symbols*** Equivalent expressions and solutions of linear equations
How Likely Is It? Probability	***Filling and Wrapping*** 3-D Measurement	***Hubcaps, Kaleidoscopes, and Mirrors!*** Transformational Geometry
Bits *and Pieces,* Part II Using Rational Numbers: Computation	***What Do You Expect?*** Probability (Expected Value)	***Samples and Populations*** Gathering data from samples to make predictions about populations
Ruins of Montarek Spatial visualization and spatial reasoning	***Data Around Us*** Number Sense	***Clever Counting*** Using trees, lists, and principals to count set: combinatorics

Example of a Problem from 6th Grade

Covering and Surrounding:
Going Around in Circles

Problem 7.2: In this problem, you will work with a collection of circular objects.

A. Use a tape measure to find the diameter and circumference of each object. Record your results in a table with these column headings:

<u>**Object**</u>   <u>**Diameter**</u>   <u>**Circumference**</u>

B. Make a coordinate graph of your data. Use the horizontal axis for diameter and the vertical axis for circumference.

C. Study your table and your graph, looking for patterns and relationships that will allow you to predict the circumference from the diameter. Test your ideas on some other circular objects. Once you think you have found a pattern, answer this question: What do you think the relationship is between the diameter and the circumference of a circle?

Mathematical and Problem Solving Goals for the Students

- To discover that it takes slightly more than 3 diameters to match the circumference of a circle.

- To use ideas about area and perimeter to solve practical problems.

Example of Informal Assessment in Teacher Materials: Summarize

Ask: Mathematicians have found a relationship between diameter and circumference. What do you think that relationship is?

Check: After the students have verbalized the relationship between the diameter and the circumference have them test out the idea on a few new circular objects.

Refine: Find the ratio of the circumference to the diameter for all the circular objects measured.

Record: In your notebooks answer the following two questions:

- How you can find the circumference of a circle if you know the diameter or the radius?

- How can you find the diameter or radius of a circle if you know the circumference?

Example of Formal Assessment:
Quiz Item

3. Given the following figures:

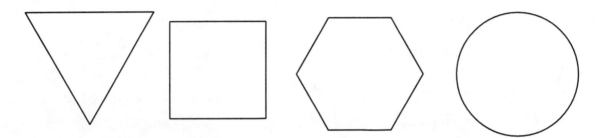

If each of the figures have a perimeter of 24 cm,

a) What is the length of the sides for each of
the polygons?

triangle _____
quadrilateral _____
hexagon _____

b) What is the diameter of the circle? _____

c) Which figure has the greatest area? _____

d) Explain how you arrived at your answer.

Example of Problem
from 7th Grade

Comparing and Scaling: The Dakotas

South and North Dakota are 45th and 46th in the U.S. in population. South Dakota has 696,000 people in 75,956 square miles; North Dakota has 639,000 people in 69,299 square miles.

Problem 5.2:

a) Which state, North Dakota or South Dakota, has the greater population density in people per square mile?

b) How many citizens of one state would have to move to the other state to make the population densities the same in both states?

Problem 5.2 Follow-Up
Find the population density of your own state. How does it compare to North and South Dakota?

Example of Problem
from 8th Grade

Thinking with Mathematical Models...
Breaking Bridges

1.1   Paper Bridges

You can do some experiments like those that engineers would do to test the strength of bridge beams and discover some of the principles involved. You can do it with a ruler, scissors, paper, and pennies as test weights.

- Cut copier paper into strips, each about 4 inches wide. Then fold the edges up about 1 inch on the long sides.

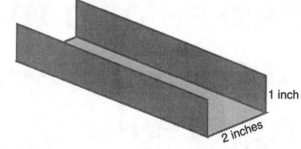

- Place the "bridge" between two books, with about 1 inch overlap on each end, and load pennies into a small paper cup at the center of the bridge until the bridge crumples.

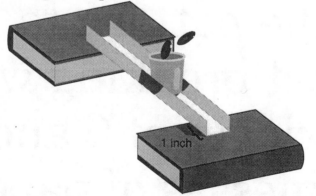

- When you find the "breaking weight" of a bridge made from one strip of paper, put two strips together to make a bridge that has double thickness. Find the breaking weight for this bridge in the same way. Then continue the experiment to find breaking weights for other thicknesses.

Problem 1.1:

Experiment to find the weight that can be carried by bridges of 1, 2, 3, 4, and 5 thicknesses of paper. Describe the pattern relating breaking weight to thickness and use the pattern to predict breaking weight for bridges of 6 and 7 thicknesses of paper.

Problem 1.1 Follow-Up

1. How would you expect the pattern in
    the results to change if you tried the
    bridge experiment with different
    material—like poster board or balsa
    wood instead of copier paper?

2. How would you expect the pattern of
    results to change if you studied the
    breaking weights of bridges with
    different lengths or widths or widths
    of folded edges?

APPENDIX C:

TECHNIQUES FOR THE LINGUISTICALLY DIVERSE CLASSROOM

Overview

Students at different levels of English proficiency successfully participate in CMP. *Moreover, limited English proficient (LEP) students receive the same content as their peers as no part of the program is diluted for them.*

Many lessons in CMP require no modification as they are already rich in comprehensible input. With these lessons, LEP students easily understand information and concepts by participating in hands-on learning activities that incorporate visuals and manipulatives. For other lessons, six simple techniques for making information comprehensible are offered. Suggested places to implement these techniques appear throughout each teacher guide; however, these should only be considered examples of when a particular technique might be appropriate.

Offering general techniques, rather than providing specific modifications, accomplishes several goals. First, CMP teacher editions do not become inundated with extraneous material unrelated to math. Second, teachers are not led to believe that cited modifications are the *only* times LEP students might need assistance -- something that may be inferred with programs limiting their modifications to space availability. Third, these general techniques acknowledge and address the wide range of English proficiency among LEP students, thus enabling teachers to present modifications at every level. Last, the combination of detailed explanations of techniques (in this section) with cited examples throughout each teacher edition provides an enrichment tutorial for teachers working with LEP students. Not only can these techniques can be used anywhere in the CMP program, but they are equally effective in all areas of the curriculum.

The Techniques

The primary guideline when developing these techniques was simplicity. Most can be implemented with no preparation; a few require minimal time to gather visual aids or props.

References to a particular technique are accompanied by a specific example related a question or section on the page. These references and examples can be found at the bottom of various pages in each teacher edition.

Initially, teachers may refer to the detailed explanations in this guide to review how to implement a referenced technique. However, due to the simplicity of these strategies, teachers will soon find references and examples in the teacher editions all they need to make specific modifications for that page. Furthermore, as teachers become familiar with these techniques, they will also begin to choose appropriate strategies for unreferenced parts of the program, as well.

A detailed explanation of each technique follows.

THE ORIGINAL REBUS TECHNIQUE

General Description
On a sheet of paper, students copy the text from all or part of a page before it is discussed. During discussion, students then generate their own rebuses for words they do not understand as the words are made comprehensible through pictures, objects, or demonstrations.

Purpose
This strategy ensures LEP students benefit from written communications in the same way as their English proficient peers. While written text summarizes key concepts, includes background information, and provides directions for completing tasks, LEP students do not often benefit from such communication.

In the past, LEP students have been traditionally paired with English proficient students, who are asked to read aloud written text. However, this approach does not provide LEP students with access to *written* communication. For example, if LEP students' sole exposure to text on a page is a one time read-aloud, then LEP students are asked to rely on memory when trying to recall the written information -- something not required of their peers. Furthermore, simply reading information aloud does not ensure that the words are made comprehensible to the LEP student. Therefore, the Original Rebus Technique offers a strategy that makes written communication meaningful to LEP students, without depending on peer cooperation or memory.

Implementation
1. Teachers identify text perceived to be difficult for LEP students to comprehend. Examples of such text may be questions appearing in Mathematical Reflections, Connections, and Applications sections of the program.

2. LEP students are asked to copy this text prior to the introduction of the page to the entire class.* The re-copied text can be handwritten, although typed versions ensure clear legibility of words. Students are instructed to leave sufficient space between lines so they have room to draw their original rebuses.

*When there's more than one LEP student in a classroom, students can take turns copying the text. Teachers can then duplicate the re-written text for all LEP students of the class, thus greatly reducing the number of times each student needs to re-copy information. Additionally, teachers can save a master copy of each re-copied text to be used with other LEP students in subsequent years.

3. LEP students receive a copy of the re-written text when the corresponding page is introduced to the class. As the information from the student book is read aloud, teachers make key words comprehensible. For example, a teacher may make the word snapshot comprehensible by showing a photo of her son.

4. After a word has been made comprehensible, the teacher writes it on the board. By doing so, LEP students can now connect the written word with a specific meaning.   At this time, LEP students create an original rebus over that key word on their sheet of paper. This rebus will then help LEP students recall the meaning of the word when referring back to the text during independent work.

Note: It is essential that LEP students draw their own rebuses. This ensures whatever symbol they choose to draw has meaning to them. The problem with providing professional or teacher-drawn rebuses is that simple drawings, by themselves, do not often convey a universal understanding of the words. For example, many English proficient students were not able to correctly identify a rebus when the word below was covered, yet could do so when they were able to view both the word and rebus. This suggests that the *written word,* not the rebus, conveyed the meaning in such situations. Moreover, by requiring LEP students to create their own rebuses, they then choose which words need to be coded. Depending on the level of English proficiency, the number of coded words can vary greatly between students.

DIAGRAM CODE TECHNIQUE

General Description
Students use a minimal number of words and drawings, diagrams, or symbols to respond to questions requiring writing.

Purpose
Learning to organize and express mathematical concepts in writing is a skill students develop over time; if LEP students are not given this same opportunity, they miss an important component of the math curriculum. Therefore, this strategy provides alternate ways for students, not yet proficient in writing English, to express mathematical thinking on paper. While their responses will not be in the same format as their English proficient peers, LEP students still have the same challenge; they must record and communicate mathematical ideas so that someone else can understand their thinking.

Implementation
1. At the beginning of the program, teachers model and encourage LEP students to use this approach when writing answers to question presented in the program.

2. To introduce how to do so, the teacher writes on the board several questions requiring written responses. These questions should be simple with obvious answers.

3. The teacher then shows the LEP students how to answer each of these questions *without writing complete sentences and paragraphs*. At the end of this session, the teacher should have modeled answering questions by using and/or combining minimal words, drawings, and diagrams. (Not every question needs to be answered by using all of these approaches.)

Note: This approach can be used for any written response in the program, but it is especially useful for responding to questions found under Mathematical Reflections. Since this part of the program provides a way to assess how well students have comprehended key concepts of the unit, this approach enables teachers to evaluate their LEP students' progress, as well.

Chart Summary Technique

General Description
This technique involves presenting information by condensing it into a pictorial chart with minimal words.

Purpose
This extension of the Diagram Code technique offers another way for LEP students to organize and express mathematical thinking with a minimal amount of writing.

Implementation
1. At the beginning of the program, the teacher shows various charts on any subject. The charts need to be simple, include pictures, and have a minimal number of words.

2. The teacher then creates and writes a question on the board that relates to each chart. For example, the teacher might show a chart of the life cycle of a plant, divided into four sections. For this chart, the teacher could create the following question: What are the growth stages of a plant?

3. The teacher continues by showing how the chart answers this question by pointing to the drawings in each section (showing the seeds, roots, stem, and flower). The teacher also points out how each section has been labeled.

4. At the end of this session, LEP students should be able to respond to a question by creating a chart with pictures and minimal words.

Note: This approach may be an alternative for LEP students when responding to some of the Unit Projects requiring detailed writing.

REBUS SCENARIO TECHNIQUE

General Description
Teachers make use of rebuses on the chalkboard during discussions and when presenting information.

Purpose
While modifications for main math concepts may be perceived as necessary for LEP students, there may be a tendency to omit such techniques for "enrichment" information (such as text appearing under Did You Know). However, if programs offer English proficient students such information, then LEP students should also have an opportunity to acquire the same knowledge. Therefore, the Rebus Scenario offers teachers a simple way to ensure all students have access to both the core and enriching aspects of the CMP program.

Implementation
1. The teacher assesses what key words may not be understood by the LEP students.

2. As each of those words are presented, the teacher simultaneously draws a rebus on the board.

Note: If there are English proficient "artists" in the classroom, teachers may opt to implement this approach is a slightly different way. Prior to the lesson, a teacher can ask an artistic student to come to the chalkboard to draw rebuses for targeted words. When using this approach, the teacher can then just point to the appropriate drawings during the lesson. If there is no time prior to a lesson, the artistic student can be asked to draw the rebuses as key words are presented. With this latter approach, it is important that students know which words to represent as rebuses and to create drawings quickly.

THE ENACTMENT TECHNIQUE

General Description
Students act out mini-scenes and use props to make information comprehensible.

Purpose
The Enactment technique ensures hypothetical scenarios presented throughout CMP are comprehended by all students. With this technique, LEP students are not excluded by from comprehending lessons involving situations reflective of "real life" scenarios.

Implementation
1. Teachers decide which simple props (if any) will enhance the enactment. These props are gathered prior to teaching the lesson.

2. At the time of the lesson, students are selected to assume the roles of characters mentioned in a CMP problem or scenario.

3. These students then pantomime and/or improvise speaking parts as they enact the written scenario presented in CMP.

Note: There may be a tendency to only select English Proficient students for mini - scene roles; however, numerous parts can also be given to LEP students. For example, roles such as pantomiming shooting baskets or pretending to ride a bicycle, can be easily enacted by LEP students. These kinds of parts do not require students to speak English and can be easily modeled.

VISUAL ENHANCEMENT TECHNIQUE

General Description
The Visual Enhancement technique uses maps, photographs, pictures in books, and objects to make information comprehensible.

Purpose
The Visual Enhancement technique makes information comprehensible by providing nonverbal input. This technique is most helpful for conveying information that is unlikely to be understood through enactment or creating rebuses. By adding pictures or real objects to lessons, LEP students have the opportunity to receive the same information presented to their English peers -- who are able understand the written text without visual aids. This approach ensures LEP students equally acquire and benefit from descriptive and/or background information sections of the program

Implementation
1. Teachers decide if information on a page is unlikely to be understood with a rebus or by having students create an enactment. For example, maps are often used with this technique to help students understand what part of the world an informative section or investigation is centered around. (In contrast, a mere rebus "outline" of the same country would not likely to be understood by anyone.) Likewise, topics such as video games, different kinds of housing, and newspaper advertisements are more easily comprehended by merely showing examples than by trying to draw something representative of the topic.

2. When teachers decide visual aids are the best approach for making information comprehensible, examples are sought prior to teaching the lesson.

3. Teachers then show the visual aid at the appropriate time during the lesson.

Note: In the first year of implementation, English proficient students can earn extra credit by finding appropriate visual aids for targeted lessons. Teachers can then keep the pictures, objects (if possible), and name of book (with page number) on file for use in subsequent years.

SUMMARY

The six techniques (Original Rebus, Diagram Code, Chart Summary, Rebus Scenario, Enactment, and Visual Enhancement) ensure LEP students receive the same math curriculum as their English proficient peers. Although each technique differs in implementation, they all offer ways for LEP students to acquire and express the mathematical ideas presented in CMP.

Last, although these approaches have been created specifically for LEP students, they can be equally effective for many Special Education students.

REFERENCES

Britton, J.N. (1970). *Language and Learning*. Coral Gables, FL: University of Miami Press, 1970.

Fey, J.T., Fitzgerald, W.M., Friel, S.N., Lappan, G.T., & Phillips, E.D. (1991). *Connected mathematics: A proposal submitted in response to the middle school materials development solicitation*. National Science Foundation Grant MDR-91-50217.

National Council of Teachers of Mathematics. *Curriculum and Evaluation Standards for School Mathematics*. Reston, VA: National Council of Teachers of Mathematics, 1989.

_____ *Professional Standards for Teaching Mathematics*. Reston, VA: National Council of Teachers of Mathematics, 1991.